I LIKE IKE

Wednesday, January 21

9
10
11
12
1
2
3
4
5

My first day at the President's Desk. Plenty of worries and difficult problems. But such has been my portion for a long time — the result is that this just seems (today) like a continuation of all I've been doing since July '41 — even before...

WESTERN UNION
W. P. MARSHALL, PRESIDENT

(13)

The filing time shown in the date line on telegrams and day letters is STANDARD TIME at point of origin. Time of receipt is STANDARD TIME at point of destination.

0A049

O VYA032 PD=TDVY ENCINO CALIF 25 1027AMP=   1955 SEP 25 PM 12 17

PRESIDENT EISENHOWER=

FITZSIMMONS ARMY HOSPITAL DVR=

YOU KNOW WHOS ON FIRST, SO MAKE THIS A FAST AND SAFE

HOME RUN. YOUR ROOTERS=

ABBOTT AND COSTELLO=

UNIVERSAL STUDIOS
UNIVERSAL CITY
CALIFORNIA

E-H-R
Camp Photographer

THE IKE FILES

Mementos of the man and his era

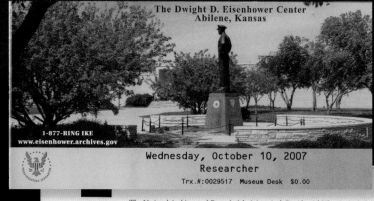

The Dwight D. Eisenhower Center
Abilene, Kansas

1-877-RING IKE
www.eisenhower.archives.gov

Wednesday, October 10, 2007
Researcher

Trx.#:0029517   Museum Desk $0.00

The National Archives and Records Administration's Presidential Libraries include:

Herbert Hoover Presidential Library, West Branch, IA
Franklin D. Roosevelt Presidential Library, Hyde Park, NY
Harry S. Truman Presidential Library, Independence, MO
Dwight D. Eisenhower Presidential Library, Abilene, KS
John F. Kennedy Presidential Library and Museum, Boston, MA
Lyndon Baines Johnson Presidential Library, Austin, TX
Gerald R. Ford Presidential Library, Ann Arbor, MI
(Museum is located in Grand Rapids, MI)
Jimmy Carter Presidential Library, Atlanta, GA
Ronald Reagan Presidential Library, Simi Valley, CA
George Bush Presidential Library, College Station, TX
William J. Clinton Presidential Library, Little Rock, AR

PRESIDENTIAL LIBRARIES

Part of the National Archives
and Records Administration
Visit online at:
http://www.archives.gov/presidential-libraries/

17740

CONTENTS

GROWING UP ON THE PLAINS 1

BETWEEN THE WARS 42

THE GREAT CHALLENGE 68

BETWEEN BIG JOBS 99

THE EISENHOWER ERA 115

AN EX-PRESIDENT 237

INDEX 260

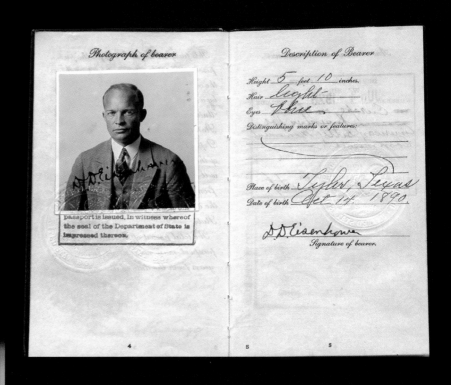

KEEPERS OF THE LEGACY

A pre-1959 version of Dwight Eisenhower's presidential seal — it contains 48 stars — is made of plaster and kept at the Eisenhower Presidential Library and Museum.

Karl Weissenbach,
Director, Eisenhower Presidential Library and Museum

Dwight D. Eisenhower died in March 1969, only about two months short of the 25th anniversary of D-Day.

In 1969, the distance in time from that world-altering event seemed vast. Yet thousands of Americans alive in 1969 – many of them only in their 40s – had personal memories of landing on the coast of Normandy on June 6, 1944, and then advancing across Europe toward victory the next year.

Almost four decades have passed since the death of Eisenhower, and every day the United States loses on average about 1,100 World War II veterans. Every day means that fewer Americans can directly recall serving under the general.

That suggests the professional challenge faced by the keepers of the general's legacy, the staff members of the Eisenhower Library and Museum in Abilene, Kansas. Not only must they maintain the records of Dwight Eisenhower's life and service, but also they must bring his story to later generations, some with no personal recollection of his crusade in Europe – or even of his two terms as president. Their job is to help visitors – serious scholars and passing tourists alike – understand the complex world faced by Eisenhower in his roles as military leader and as statesman.

Almost every adult with a driver's license can appreciate the impact of the interstate highway system.

It was initiated by Dwight D. Eisenhower when he was president. Almost every American, then, should find remarkable the poor conditions he encountered as he led a motor convoy across the United States just after World War I. That long trip over a patchwork of bumpy paths and dusty roads set him thinking about the importance to the country of a first-class highway system. The Eisenhower Presidential Library contains photographs of the conditions faced on that transcontinental journey. They convey the bumpy reality in ways modern drivers can understand.

Almost every American understands the challenge that race has posed through our country's history. The struggle by minorities for fairness and equality accelerated in Eisenhower's two terms as president, and for years the conventional wisdom has held that he was less than fervent – timid in the mind of one historian – in his efforts on behalf of civil rights.

Yet the evidence in Abilene suggests that that is a simplistic view. Handwritten notes made by the president before he addressed the nation on television about the Central High School desegregation controversy of 1957 show him balancing a belief in the bedrock rights of Americans with his specific constitutional responsibilities as president. The result: To the relief of the black students' families and to the chagrin of segregationists throughout the American South, he deployed members of the Army's 101st Airborne Division to enforce a federal court order. Black students were allowed

to go to class at Central High School. Whatever the residents of Little Rock thought about President Eisenhower's conclusion, it's likely none of them thought it indecisive.

At the Eisenhower Presidential Library and Museum, the archivists' task begins with careful preservation of the physical record, maintaining the public and private papers, the photographs and the artifacts that document Eisenhower's life and the times he knew. Once processed, they are made available to scholars and students of the era, and some of those artifacts are displayed in the museum for the public to see.

This book showcases those invaluable symbols of a remarkable American life. Many have never been seen by most Americans.

The world has changed in a thousand small ways since 1969. That year, the ailing former president watched on closed-circuit television as grandson David Eisenhower was married to Julie Nixon. As the ceremony proceeded, granddad remarked that he disapproved of the grandson's haircut. Short by the standards of many of David's contemporaries, the younger Eisenhower's hair remained far too long for the world his grandfather had known. What Dwight D. Eisenhower would think of American popular culture today is impossible to know.

The interest today's Americans have in him in retrospect is easier to gauge. The growing number of visitors and scholars who travel to Abilene is our barometer of that.

INTRODUCTION

Just north of Andrew Johnson; south of Chester Alan Arthur. In 1962 those were the coordinates for anyone looking to find Dwight Eisenhower in a historians' ranking of 31 American presidents. In that group Eisenhower stood 22nd — at least according to the historians who were asked.

His company is more distinguished today.

In 1981 another group of historians ranked Eisenhower 12th. In 1982, he placed 11th in one poll and ninth in another. By 1996 he sat solidly in ninth place, between Andrew Jackson and James Madison. In a 2000 C-Span poll Eisenhower again finished ninth. Among leadership qualities, his highest ranking was in "moral authority," where he finished fifth — right behind Franklin Roosevelt, Theodore Roosevelt, Abraham Lincoln and George Washington.

That top-tier status endures today. In Wall Street terms, Dwight Eisenhower represents a once-overlooked blue-chip with strong fundamentals, rediscovered by investors.

According to many historians, the revolution in thinking about the 34th president results from the Eisenhower Presidential Library's rapid opening of the highest-level presidential papers, beginning in 1975. By the 1980s, historians had gained new perspective. The 1950s and 1960s caricature of Eisenhower as a rather disengaged and golf-obsessed chief executive was re-drawn.

The process continues in Abilene. In 2007 alone, the Eisenhower Library hosted more than 700 researchers. Their work, along with the continual expansion of the library's holdings, arguably influences how Americans view Eisenhower and his time. The notion of Eisenhower as a hands-off president is being overtaken by a new perspective. In fact, the 34th president was fully engaged. He grappled personally with the most sensitive and controversial issues the White House faced.

In a symposium on the 1950s that took place in 1980 at the Eisenhower Library, Thomas C. Reeves, a University of Wisconsin-Parkside scholar and biographer of Joseph McCarthy, contended that the Eisenhower era remained largely undiscovered.

"They have tons of stuff they haven't even opened yet," he said.

The succeeding two decades-plus — and the work of Eisenhower Library staff members — have proved Reeves prophetic.

When the Eisenhower Library opened for research in 1966, text holdings totaled about 12 million pages. Thanks to an active solicitation program over the years, the library in 2007 held about 26 million pages. Those holdings were expected to continue to grow; donations of historical materials brought the library 80,000 pages in 2007 alone.

Today, the library maintains an active declassification program and about 418,000 formerly classified pages have been made available to researchers. (About 350,000 pages still are considered to be potentially classified. These documents must be reviewed in accordance with statutory guidelines).

Meanwhile, the Eisenhower Presidential Library and Museum is becoming more active in public programming. One reason is the importance placed on civic education by the National Archives and Records Administration, the federal arm through which the presidential library system operates. Another reason has been the joint effort by the Library and the Eisenhower Foundation — the nonprofit support group that solicits money for the Eisenhower Center — to highlight the institution on the cultural map of Kansas and the country.

Presidential libraries generally do not receive federal funds for special events, public and educational programs or exhibits. That's the primary task of the Eisenhower Foundation.

The observance of D-Day's 50th anniversary in 1994 fit that description. Among the participants were paratrooper Wallace Strobel, who's in a familiar photograph of Eisenhower visiting troops the day before the invasion; Lord David Montgomery, son of Sir Bernard Law Montgomery, British field marshal: John Howard, a former British Army major, and Hans von Luck, German commander of the 125th Regiment of the 21st Panzer Division, which was trying to fight off the Normandy landings.

A photograph of von Luck assisting Howard, who that weekend was using a wheelchair, appeared in newspapers around the world.

That observance in 1994 occurred as the generation of veterans who fought World War II, after decades of reticence, figured it was time to describe their experiences. Four years afterward broadcast journalist Tom Brokaw published *The Greatest Generation*, a celebration of World War II veterans. The book's title struck just the right note to describe the heroic men and women who endured the Great Depression and then won World War II.

In 2002, the 50th anniversary of Eisenhower's election as president, George H.W. and Barbara Bush helped dedicate the renovated Dwight D. Eisenhower Presidential Gallery. The exhibit represented a state-of-the-art response to the challenge that the Eisenhower Library and Museum staff members faced: gaining the attention of an American public that increasingly had no personal memory of the 34th president.

The gallery, funded by $3.2 million raised by the Eisenhower Foundation, showcased exhibits and provided new interpretation of not only the Eisenhower Administration from 1953 through 1961, but also the cultural context in which it occurred.

In 2007, the 50th anniversary of the Central High School integration drama in Little Rock, Arkansas, prompted two new books devoted to Eisenhower's civil rights policies. The result was an increased understanding of a president who – although sometimes thought to have neglected taking moral leadership – nevertheless was determined to respond in a way he believed appropriate to his office. Eventually, Eisenhower deployed the 101st Airborne to enforce the court order for Central High to admit black students.

There was another phenomenon that awakened appreciation of the man.

Many commentators – remarking upon the 2007 publication of *Ike: An American Hero* by Michael Korda – welcomed a new appreciation of the competence that Eisenhower represented and the shrewd intelligence that his contemporaries may have discounted, distracted perhaps by his 100-watt smile.

Perhaps, if the Watergate era produced a nostalgia for the 33rd president, Harry Truman, and his reputation for personal integrity, so too had the perilous times of the early 21st century prompted a collective new regard for the resolve of the 34th president, who fought the Cold War yet kept his country at peace.

For those sharing that sentiment, there is Abilene, Kansas.

As the president who signed the Presidential Libraries Act in 1955, Eisenhower endorsed the concept of presidential libraries. He also personally approved the intent of the Eisenhower Foundation, which opened in 1954 a museum as a memorial to all who served in World War II, and then began to collect donations for the modern presidential library dedicated on May 1, 1962.

You're about to sample the Eisenhower Library

and Museum in the context of this fascinating man's life. In these pages, you'll find reproduced a large-type copy of Eisenhower's "military industrial complex" speech from 1961, evidently the one used by the president in his televised farewell address to the country. You'll see phrases underlined – by the president himself – and get a vivid personal perspective on the man.

You'll read letters written by the young Dwight Eisenhower to girlfriends in early 20th-century Abilene. They show him to be a lively, ambitious and occasionally anxious young man virtually unrecognizable from the mature general and chief executive many Americans recall today.

These historical jewels and many others have been organized and preserved by a trained staff ready to make them available to scholars or anyone else expressing a wish to see them. They await contemporary students ready to investigate the historical figure, and perhaps ready to admire the man their grandparents so liked.

Meanwhile, the collections await you. Read on.

— Brian Burnes

a picture of one of the wolf hunts I is going to be one next Sat. I

His hand on a sapling and a firearm perched on his shoulder, 17-year-old Dwight Eisenhower of Abilene, Kansas, stood with more than a dozen fellow hunters and onlookers as they posed for a photographer in the early 1900s. The occasion, Eisenhower wrote, was a wolf hunt, but the prey was more likely coyotes. Wolves lived in Kansas in the 19th century, and farmers and ranchers organized large hunts to remove them, but the last wolf in the state was reported in 1905. This photograph was made into a postcard and in May 1908, Eisenhower mailed it to a friend in Manhattan, Kansas, mentioning also a baseball game in which "I made a rank error."

GROWING UP ON THE PLAINS

The year 1890, according to historian Frederick Jackson Turner, was when the American frontier closed. For the family of David and Ida Eisenhower, the occasion passed without notice. They were practicing a way of life closer to the frontier than the modern world.

The Eisenhowers had married in a small town near Abilene, Kansas, in 1885. A few years later they fell on hard times and David found railroad work, which took the family briefly to Texas.

In 1890, in Denison, Texas, Dwight Eisenhower was born. He was the Eisenhowers' third child, all sons. A year later, David and Ida Eisenhower returned to Kansas, settling in Abilene. There they stayed.

In Abilene, days began at 5 a.m. Before heading for school the Eisenhower boys were expected to do the chores. For Dwight, that meant feeding chickens, gathering eggs and milking cows. The family home was heated by a stove and the Eisenhower family did not have running water,

tended. There
iles north, 54-08,

We will probably
play the college
again next mon,
they beat us in
a five inning game
the other day,
7=3. I made a rank
error, Young Ike.

Mr. Orin Snider,
Manhattan,
Kansas.
1104 moro St.

so laundry days meant carrying water heated by the same stove.

"Some mornings were worse than others," Dwight wrote decades later. "On washdays, all white clothes were boiled to kill germs. While one of us turned the washing machine, the others brought in water for heating in the reservoir, a tank holding five gallons, built as an integral part of a cookstove. No burden weighs more than a bucket of water on a boy's arm, unless he is carrying one in each hand."

At the turn of the 20th century, Abilene was about 30 years removed from its uninhibited frontier days, when it was briefly the terminus of the Kansas Pacific Railroad and "Wild" Bill Hickok patrolled as marshal. There were saloons and occasional gunplay, just as in the movies. In the 1948 film "Red River," in which John Wayne and Montgomery Clift settled accounts during a difficult cattle drive, Abilene was the ultimate destination of the trail ride.

Horse-and-buggy days in Abilene. Several generations of Eisenhower's family had called Kansas home.

Dwight Eisenhower, left, and his brothers at the first home the family occupied, after they returned to Abilene from Texas.

"Texas cattlemen, after the Civil War, sought eastern markets," Eisenhower later wrote. "In 1869, they started to drive their herds into Abilene, the nearest railhead. Our national folk heroes were a fairly riotous breed even in the best of times and cowboys coming in off the long, lonely trails were starved for home-cooked food, and more especially for drink, for excitement and amusement."

Young Dwight came of age in a different Abilene.

"Almost as a reaction to the violent early days," Eisenhower later wrote, "the town usually seemed extraordinarily peaceful and quiet."

His paternal grandparents had been attracted to Abilene in the late 1870s by news accounts of cheap land. They had been members of the River Brethren denomination of Pennsylvania.

After David Jacob and Ida Elizabeth Stover Eisenhower were married, David's father gave him a plot of land, which David mortgaged so he could become a partner in a general store. The venture failed, taking with it most of David and Ida's resources.

After his stint with the railroad in Texas, David found work back in Abilene as a mechanic in the Belle Springs Creamery. Dwight's parents eventually acquired a home on South Fourth Street when an uncle, a veterinarian named Abraham Lincoln Eisenhower, sold it to pursue missionary work.

Living there would not have been easy. In addition to Dwight and his older brothers, Arthur and Edgar, the family grew to include Roy, Paul,

In the earliest picture of him known to have survived, Dwight Eisenhower, lower right, posed with his brothers for a studio photographer in Topeka, Kansas.

Earl and Milton (Paul died in infancy). All those boys eventually squeezed into a house that Eisenhower once estimated had less square footage than the Pentagon office he occupied after World War II.

Still, there was money enough at least for a trip to Topeka to pose the young family for a photographer. Decades later, after his presidency, Eisenhower didn't remember his Abilene days as wanting.

"We had been poor, but one of the glories of America at the time was that we didn't know it," he wrote in 1963. "It was a good, secure small-town life, and that we wanted for luxuries didn't occur to any of us."

Dwight, front row, second from left, couldn't dress as nicely as his fellow pupils.

In 1902, the Eisenhowers sat for a family portrait. Father David appeared serious, as always, and mother Ida looked as if she was about to break into her customary smile. From left in the second row were Dwight, Edgar, Earl, Arthur, and Roy. Between the parents was Milton.

Below: A keepsake owned by David and Ida.

Outfitted in over-alls, teenaged Dwight Eisenhower sat with his pals on a camping trip, probably in the early 1900s.

In the early 1830s, young Abraham Lincoln wrestled a local champion named Jack Armstrong in New Salem, Ill. By 1860, when Lincoln was running for president, a campaign biography circulated the story and the match became legend. Although Lincoln's fight might have been embellished, depending on the source, the point concerned how a future president won the hearts of locals by his courage and strength.

Presidential historians like to describe another fight years later, perhaps 1903, featuring another future president. This fight took place in Abilene. It involved a teenaged Dwight Eisenhower, who was from the south side of the railroad tracks, and Wes Merrifield, who was from the north side. Some accounts say the two fought for an hour, others for two hours. Most biographies describe the outcome as a draw; each fighter, exhausted, conceded he could not lick the other.

Whatever the facts, the event was a glimpse into the boyhood of Dwight Eisenhower and into one certain reality of young Eisenhower's life: class.

The railroad tracks, which ran east and west through Abilene, served in the local consciousness as a line between haves and have-nots.

Older brother Edgar Eisenhower recalled how he and Dwight sold the family's produce to residents of north Abilene neighborhoods. The north-siders, Edgar said, "made us feel like beggars." That slight, Edgar added, "made us scrappers."

Young people in turn-of-the-century Abilene apparently honored protocols of turf, patrolling the perimeters and occasionally deriding those who strayed across.

Sometimes that included young Dwight.

In 1903, Dwight entered the seventh grade at Garfield Junior High School. Abilene had two grade schools – one on the south side and one on the north – but only one junior high and one high school. Attending Garfield meant the mingling of north and south Abilene.

Today, the long battle between Eisenhower and Merrifield suggests tenacity and toughness on the part of both youths. According to presidential historian Michael Beschloss, the young Eisenhower may have had to learn those characteristics.

Once, the young Dwight ran home to avoid a fight. When Eisenhower's father heard about it, Beschloss wrote, his father sent him back to stand up for himself.

Abilene, Kans,
Feb. 27, 1905.

Dear Cousin:—

You will see from the date on my letter that I am slow. I received your letter two or three days ago and one thing you said in it was unlucky. You know you said I must not get sick. Well I've got the worst sore throat that I ever had or ever hope to see again. Milton asked for the picture you sent me and I let him have it and he said, "This looks like Nettie, is it her?" Milton is much better but very weak and cannot walk. This old paper hasn't any lines and I feel miserable. Three boys came down there to the Reform School from here for chicken stealing. I have not started to school yet. Arthur intends to go to Kansas City in a few days. He is going to work at short hand. If Uncle Clarence and Aunt Alice don't go before March 9th tell them to stop and visit here awhile because we will not be quarenteened aft-er March 9. I'll bet this writing would take a prize any where and

"This old paper hasn't any lines and I feel miserable." Eisenhower wrote his cousin, N. Stover Jackson, about his sore throat. The ailment was far from the worst of his health worries in those years.

Eisenhower's perspective on his high school years was sometimes grim.

"The most dramatic difference between high schools of today and those of my time," he wrote in the 1960s, "is probably not in the curriculum but in the life expectancy of the students."

Early in his high school career a mysterious ailment threatened, if not his life, his leg. Running down a wooden platform in his freshman year, Eisenhower fell and evidently skinned his knee. There was no bleeding, just a red spot.

He forgot about it until the next day when he sank onto his mother's sofa, suddenly fatigued. Then he faded into incoherence. For two weeks, Eisenhower slipped into and out of a coma.

The illness confounded doctors, who thought it was blood poisoning. An infection appeared to be spreading from his leg to his groin and abdomen. Eisenhower – then 14 – heard one doctor mention amputation. He begged his parents and his older brother Edgar to resist. He

would rather die, he said, than not be able to play baseball or football.

"I could not imagine an existence in which I was not playing one or both," he recalled. At one point Edgar slept across the threshold to the room where his brother slept, just in case.

Doctors ultimately treated the ailment by painting carbolic acid on his body. Whatever the illness was, it receded and the threat of amputation disappeared. Eisenhower missed enough school that he had to repeat an academic year.

For some subjects in high school, Eisenhower was an enthusiastic student. As a young man, he loved history. When his mother found that he was neglecting other school work as well as household chores, she locked his history books

Abilene High School: Dwight sat in the front row, second from right.

Athletics

By Dwight Eisenhower

Early in the fall of 1908, the High School boys organized an Athletic Association for the year. After electing Dwight Eisenhower president, Harry Makins vice-president and Herbert Sommers secretary and treasurer, we proceeded to do business.

Deciding not to play any base ball in the fall, we started on football at once. Bruce Hurd was elected captain, and soon a large number of candidates for the squad were out working. After two weeks of hard work, Captain Hurd decided on the following team:

Left end	Huffman
Left tackle	Ingersoll
Left guard	Pattin
Center	Funk
Right guard	Weckle
Right tackle	Hurd
Right end	D. Eisenhower
Quarter	Merrifield
Left half	Makins
Right half	Sommers
Full back	E. Eisenhower

We were deprived of our coach, but nevertheless, turned out a very creditable team. Unfortunately, however, only four games were played during the season, not giving the team a chance to prove its ability. But for the games that were played, the students supported the team loyally, and time and again the boys surmounted great difficulties, cheered on by the fierce enthusiasm displayed by our rooters.

After the football season closed, we had to spend the winter dreaming of past victories and future glories, for A. H. S. boasts of no indoor gymnasium, and basket ball was never played here. But we improved the condition of the Association itself, by drawing up a constitution, which makes the organization a permanent one, and each year it will be simply a question of electing new officers.

Thanking the citizens of the town who have taken such an interest in the High School Athletics, and also our fellow classmates for their loyalty to us, we are yours for future victories on the gridiron by teams of dear old A. H. S.

FOOTBALL SCHEDULE

Abilene vs. Junction City at Junction City.
Abilene vs. Junction City at Abilene.
Abilene vs. Chapman at Abilene.
Abilene vs. Agricultural College at Abilene.

— THE VAULTER —

His battle against even the suggestion of amputation showed how much sports meant to the young Dwight Eisenhower. More evidence: as a student at Abilene High School, he and his buddies organized an athletic association and he was chosen president.

Facing page; "Big" and "Little" Ikes graduated the same year from Abilene High School. Dwight was named David Dwight at birth, but was called Dwight to avoid mix-ups with his father. Later, he transposed his first and middle names.

in a closet. Later, Eisenhower found the key and smuggled the volumes out. In the 1909 yearbook, he was described as the best historian and mathematician of his graduating class at Abilene High School.

According to the class prophecy, Dwight would become a history professor at Yale University. His brother Edgar, it said, would become president of the United States.

EDGAR NEWTON
EISENHOWER

♣

"Big Ike" is the greatest football player of the class. Also on his head there is a depression due to non-development of the conscious and over-development of the sub-conscious brain. Football teams '07, '08, '09. Base ball teams '07, '08, '09; captain '08.

DAVID DWIGHT
EISENHOWER

♣

"Little Ike," now a couple inches taller than "big Ike," is our best historian and mathematician. President of Athletic Association, '09; Football, '07, '08; Baseball '08, '09.

Dwight Eisenhower graduated from Abilene High School in 1909 at the age of 18 alongside his brother. The 20-year-old Edgar had dropped out of school after his father reproved him for poor grades, and he went to work at the Belle Springs Creamery in Abilene. He returned in time to graduate with Dwight, who had to make up some time himself after suffering a serious illness.

Then both boys went to work to finance Edgar's future enrollment at the University of Michigan. The understanding was that Dwight would join his older brother on the Ann Arbor campus in two years.

In the first summer after high school, Dwight worked on a farm and then at a small company that made steel grain bins while Edgar worked at the creamery. By the time Edgar left for Michigan Dwight was working at the creamery. He eventually became second engineer in the creamery's ice plant, which was almost literally a full-time job – 84 hours a week, seven days from 6 a.m. to 6 p.m., 52 weeks a year, at $90 a month. The young Dwight entertained thoughts of going to Michigan himself, and perhaps playing football there.

But an Abilene friend, Everett "Swede" Hazlett, put a different idea into Eisenhower's head: take the exam required for entrance into one of the country's military service academies. Perhaps, Hazlett told Eisenhower, he could play football for Navy. At any rate, his college education could be paid by the government.

Eisenhower turned into a serious student. He frequented the offices of Joseph Howe, who edited a weekly newspaper. Eisenhower borrowed books and read out-of-town papers. In October 1910, he took the service academy exam over two days in Topeka. Of eight candidates, his scores were the second highest.

In November 1910, U.S. Sen. Joseph Bristow of Kansas informed Eisenhower that he had been appointed to West Point. He left for the academy the next summer.

An informal family portrait made in 1910, when the 20-year-old Eisenhower won appointment to the U.S. Military Academy.

June 9th 1911

On his way by train to West Point for his first year, Eisenhower stopped in Chicago to visit an old friend from Abilene, Ruby Norman. He would not return to civilian life for four decades, and then it was to run for president.

WEST POINT

Standing proudly for the photographer, West Point cadet Dwight D. Eisenhower personified the regimented routine at the U.S. Military Academy. The clipboard on the mantel behind him suggested that, in Eisenhower's time, each minute at the academy was present and accounted for.

Yet for all the rigid spine the young Eisenhower showed on occasion, there were plenty of times when he grew impatient with cadet protocol.

The rules, for instance, forbade smoking.

"So," Eisenhower once wrote, "I started smoking cigarettes."

In a celebrated instance Eisenhower and a fellow cadet, found guilty of an infraction, were ordered to report to a cadet corporal either in "full-dress coats," or complete dress uniform. They responded wearing their coats – and nothing else.

Decades after his time at West Point, Eisenhower requested a summary of the demerits he received. Taken from the military academy's "abstract of delinquencies," the list filled several pages, and appeared to document the career of a sad-sack cadet.

In his first year, 1911, Eisenhower had problems with punctuality. He appeared late at breakfast and parade and chapel and drill formation.

Other offenses through 1915: leaving his room "in disorder" (2 demerits); deploying a dirty field bayonet (2 demerits); having shoes under his bed not properly shined (1 demerit); "wearing very dirty white trousers" (2 demerits); "gazing about in ranks while marching in parade" (2 demerits); passing plates in a "careless and improper manner" (2 demerits); being asleep in chair at inspection (2 demerits).

The summary made special note of a violation of rules on dancing; he spun his partner so fast that her ankle showed. Eisenhower was confined to barracks for all of September 1913.

In later years, Eisenhower allowed that he "looked with distaste on classmates whose days and nights were haunted by fear of demerits and low grades."

Perhaps he didn't believe he had time to worry about such things, or was too old to care. When he arrived in West Point, New York, in June 1911, Eisenhower was close to 21 years old.

Facing page: Rigid cadet, not-so-rigid obedience: a tinted photo of young Eisenhower and part of a typewritten summary of his demerits, prepared decades later.

1911 (4th Class)

15 July   Relieved from post by permission at 7:35 a.m., 11th instant (no delinquency). Orderly board not properly posted during parade, July 14. 1 demerit. Tarnished rod in cartridge box at parade. 1 demerit.

20 July   Absent at 8 a.m. drill formation. 3 demerits.

30 July   Overshoes not arranged as prescribed at retreat. 1 demerit.

2 August   Dirty gun and collar not properly adjusted at parade. 4 demerits. Overshoes not in prescribed position during parade. 1 demerit.

A CONFIDANTE

At West Point, Dwight Eisenhower would be a football star and a yell leader. Occasionally, he would be a sourpuss, too. You'll find it in his own words, in letters he wrote to Ruby Norman, an Abilene girlfriend in whom Eisenhower clearly felt comfortable confiding.

"Seems like I'm never cheerful any more," he wrote early in his Military Academy career. "The fellows that used to call me 'Sunny Jim' call me 'Gloomy Face' now…."

In 1916, serving at Fort Sam Houston in San Antonio, Texas, Eisenhower's lot didn't seem much improved.

"My life here, is, in the main uninteresting – nothing much doing – and I get tired of the same old grind some times," he wrote Ruby that January.

After high school, Ruby, a musician, toured in a six-member orchestra, "The All-American Girls." She studied at the Chicago Conservatory of Music and in 1911, when Eisenhower traveled through Chicago on the way to his first year at West Point, he stopped to visit her. She took a snapshot of him on the sidewalk.

For the rest of his life Dwight stayed friendly with Ruby, who eventually married another Abilene acquaintance, Ralph Lucier.

One historian tells how Eisenhower, campaigning for president in 1952, recognized his old chum from the train when it stopped at Warsaw, Indiana. He invited her aboard and introduced her to his wife, Mamie, who later wrote that the meeting "was ever so much more pleasant than what the movies lead us to expect."

The correspondence between Dwight and Ruby stretched through 1967, when she died in St. Louis of leukemia.

According to a letter written to Eisenhower by a daughter, Ruby spent some of her last days in her St. Louis hospital room, laughing out loud at portions of *At Ease*, the 1967 memoir by Eisenhower, who had sent it to her.

"This is the first book that really sounds like Dwight," she said. She would know, considering the letters he had started writing her more than 50 years before.

RUBY GRACE NORMAN

"I have that love for music in my veins,
And glory in the violin's sweet strains."

When her musical ambitions are realized, the world as well as A. H. S. will know her value.

Music loomed large in Ruby Norman's life, according to the Abilene High School yearbook. A string player, after graduation she toured with an all-female musical group.

Dwight D. Eisenhower

Lieutenant United States Army

WEST POINT
NOV 5 1913
N.Y.

Miss Ruby Norman,

Clayton,

Alabama.

Jr. Lewis Concert Co.

UNITED STATES MILITARY ACADEMY
WEST POINT, NEW YORK

Dear Little Girl:

The last time you wrote you hopped onto me because you had written twice before getting a letter from me. Well, I'm just calling your attention to the fact that this is the third I've written since I received one.

Next Sat. is the Navy game. In case I don't write for several weeks following that game - please don't think that it's on account of indifference or anything like that. If we win I'll probably be writing you on every day. That probably a poor way to get you to write for the Army too, but you had better, if you don't want your head punched PF.

Cadet Eisenhower compared notes with his chum Ruby Norman. Who had written whom more often?

GETTING BY AT THE ACADEMY

The West Point class of 1915 later was described as the one "the stars fell on." Of the 115 graduates who served in World War II, more than half earned the rank of general. Two of them, Dwight Eisenhower and Omar Bradley, became five-star generals.

One of them became president.

Given all that, Eisenhower's career at West Point was decidedly mixed.

At graduation, he ranked 61st of 164. In discipline he stood 125th. In his memoir, *At Ease*, Eisenhower wondered why he hadn't taken his studies more seriously. He also conceded that, after a 1912 knee injury ended his collegiate athletics career, his morale declined.

"I was almost despondent and several times had to be prevented from resigning by the persuasive efforts of classmates," he wrote.

Over time Eisenhower began to view his West Point experience differently. He would, for example, recall June 14, 1911 – the day he and his fellow classmates were sworn in as cadets – in an almost cinematic way.

"Whatever had gone before, it was a supreme moment," he wrote. "The United States of America would now and henceforth mean something different than it ever had before. From here on it would be the nation I would be serving, not myself.

"Suddenly the flag itself meant something. Across half a century, I can look back and see a raw-boned, gawky Kansas boy from the farm country, earnestly repeating the words that would make him a cadet."

And yet – also in *At Ease* – he admitted bewilderment.

"From the first day at West Point, and any number of times thereafter, I often asked myself: What am I doing here? Like the other young men, I sometimes wondered – where did I come from, by what route and why; by what chance arrangement of fate did I come by this uniform?"

Eisenhower's biographers have described his West Point performance as inconsistent, both accomplished and middling.

Stephen Ambrose suggested that the institution's lock-step intellectual approach disappointed the former Abilene High School scholar who had gained a reputation for enjoying history.

"English was composition, never literature," Ambrose wrote. "History was fact, never inquiry."

Eisenhower also didn't show much enthusiasm for West Point ritual. After surviving the hazing then dealt out to plebes at the academy, Eisenhower rarely looked for revenge against the plebes who entered after him.

"Most new upperclassmen took great pleasure in doling out the harassment they had received as plebes," wrote Eisenhower biographer Carlo D'Este. "Eisenhower was an exception and was never comfortable in the role of the tormentor."

A return trip to Abilene in 1913 allowed

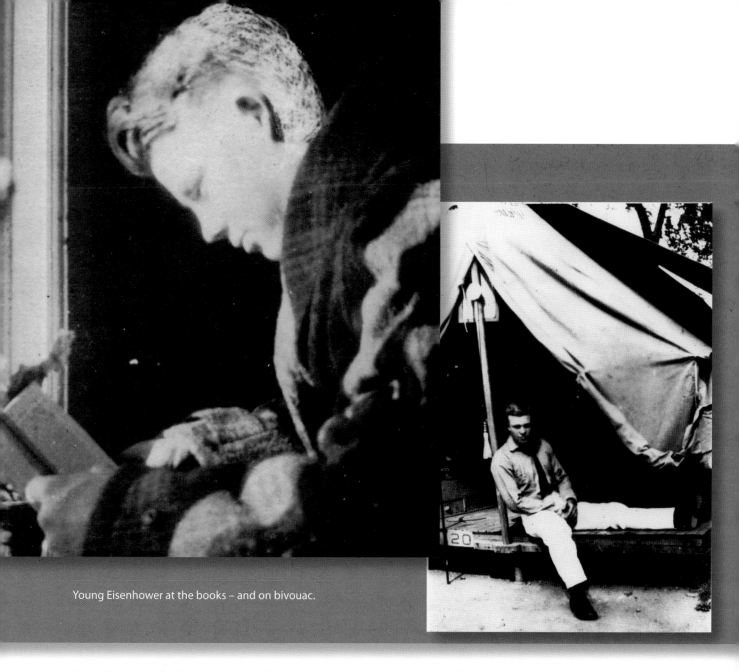

Young Eisenhower at the books – and on bivouac.

Eisenhower to bask in accomplishment. He wore his summer whites around town and told of playing football against the great Jim Thorpe. Wes Merrifield, the Abilene north-sider whom Eisenhower had faced in a celebrated street fight years before, told him he didn't want a re-match.

And when Eisenhower wrote Abilene friend Ruby Norman, he included a card bearing both his name and that of the academy, and allowed how "West Point, N.Y., looks awfully nice as an address on an envelope."

Eisenhower never forgot that his education at West Point was financed by the federal government. To someone who had taken Abilene jobs after high school to help pay for the University of Michigan education of his older brother, this meant something.

Getting an education, he once noted, "when you don't have to pay for it when I'd been working for two years to help my brother....Well, I thought this was a wonderful thing."

Mark Clark, a West Point classmate who also became a general and who several times visited Eisenhower not long before his death at Walter Reed Army Hospital in Washington in 1969, remembered what Eisenhower most wanted to discuss –West Point.

"Not about being president, not about being supreme commander, about D-Day, none of that," Clark said. "West Point was all, ever."

In Eisenhower's senior year, *The Howitzer* yearbook poked fun at cadet life with cartoons, right, and at the graduates with a few obscure, mocking references, facing page.

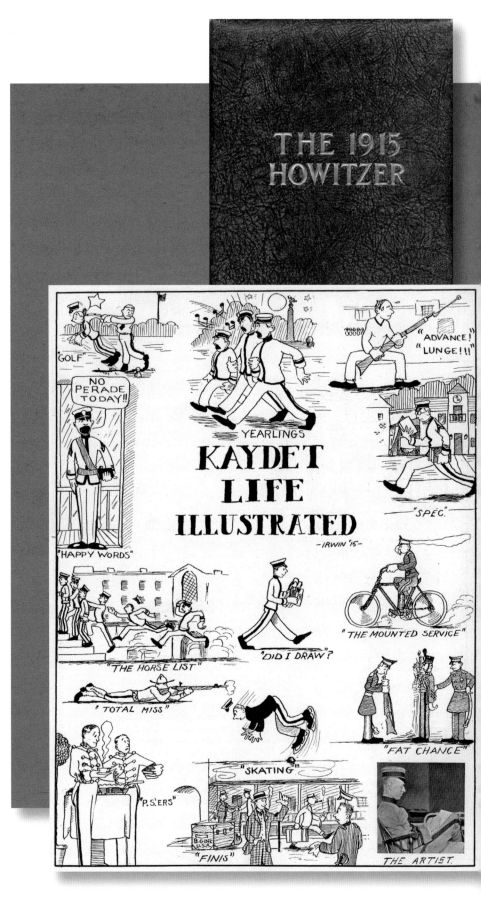

DWIGHT DAVID EISENHOWER

ABILENE, KANSAS

Senatorial Appointee, Kansas

"Ike"

Corporal, Sergeant, Color Sergeant; A.B., B.A., Sharpshooter; Football Squad (3, 2), "A" in Football; Baseball Squad (4); Cheer Leader; Indoor Meet (4, 3).

"Now, fellers, it's just like this. I've been asked to say a few words this evening about this business. Now, me and Walter Camp, we think—"
— *Himself*

THIS is Señor Dwight David Eisenhower, gentlemen, the terrible Swedish-Jew, as big as life and twice as natural. He claims to have the best authority for the statement that he is the handsomest man in the Corps and is ready to back up his claim at any time. At any rate you'll have to give it to him that he's well-developed abdominally—and more graceful in pushing it around than Charles Calvert Benedict. In common with most fat men, he is an enthusiastic and sonorous devotee of the King of Indoor Sports, and roars homage at the shrine of Morpheus on every possible occasion.

However, the memory of man runneth back to the time when the little Dwight was but a slender lad of some 'steen years, full of joy and energy and craving for life and movement and change. 'Twas then that the romantic appeal of West Point's glamour grabbed him by the scruff of the neck and dragged him to his doom. Three weeks of Beast gave him his fill of life and movement and as all the change was locked up at the Cadet Store out of reach, poor Dwight merely consents to exist until graduation shall set him free.

At one time he threatened to get interested in life and won his "A" by being the most promising back in Eastern football—but the Tufts game broke his knee and the promise. Now Ike must content himself with tea, tiddledywinks and talk, at all of which he excels. Said prodigy will now lead us in a long, loud yell for— Dare Devil Dwight, the Dauntless Don.

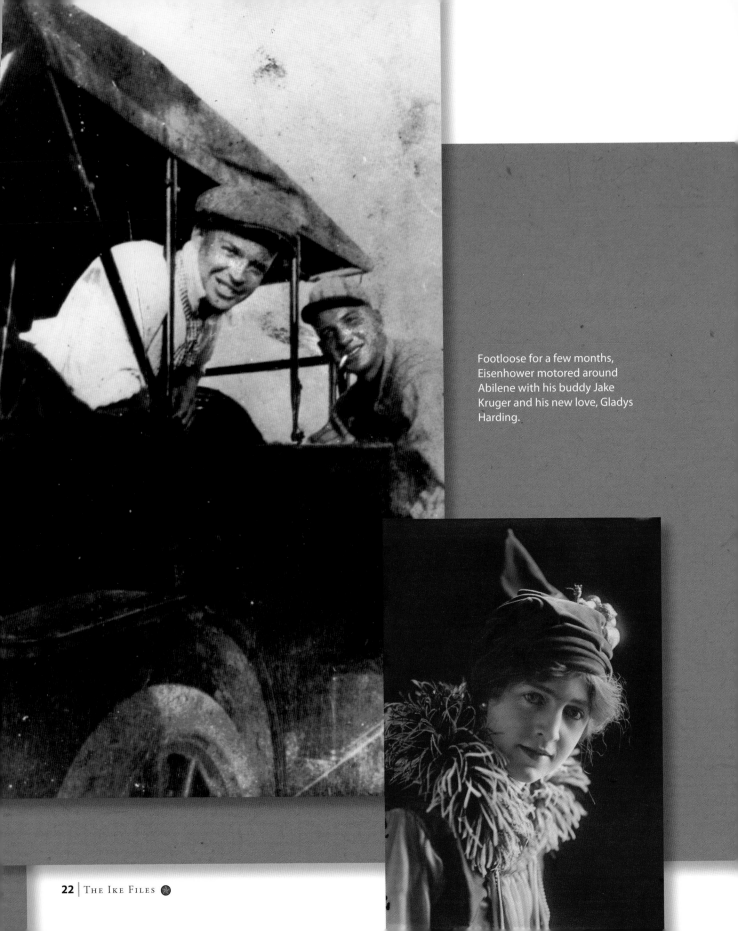

Footloose for a few months, Eisenhower motored around Abilene with his buddy Jake Kruger and his new love, Gladys Harding.

In the universal language of recent college graduates, Dwight Eisenhower was between things in 1915.

He had graduated from West Point, and had received his commission and his assignment to report to Fort Sam Houston that fall in San Antonio, Texas.

For a brief time, after four years of the regimented service-academy life, he could wear his cap at a jaunty tilt and take a ragtop out on the road. It's something of a revelation to Americans who remember the 34th president as an aging paragon of rectitude and resolve.

In summer 1915 he was utterly human. He spent much of that summer with Gladys Harding and wound up falling in love, according to historian Stephen Ambrose.

"Your love is my whole world," Ike wrote her. "Nothing else counts at all.

"I want to hear you say the three words more than I ever have," he proclaimed in a letter on Aug. 18. "For, girl, I do love you and want you to know it."

Like Ruby Norman, Gladys Harding was a touring musician, but that summer was free for her and Eisenhower. Harding kept a detailed diary of her activities, and many times recorded Dwight Eisenhower arriving at her home and taking her to the movies.

"Dwight came down," she wrote on July 15. "Went to picture show. Had some beer then. J Kruger with us."

Sunday, August 8: "Dwight came down."

Monday, August 9: "Dwight came down in eve. Went to picture show."

Tuesday August 10: "Dwight came down. Went to picture show."

Wednesday, August 11: "Dwight came down. We went auto riding with Jake - then to picture show."

Saturday, August 28: "Last day at home. D came down in eve. Auto riding with he & Jake. Had some beer. Sad eve."

Apparently Harding kept Eisenhower at a distance and may have told him that her career as a musician came before romance.

In a letter to Ruby Norman five months afterward, Eisenhower promised to tell Ruby about the new woman in his life, the one he was dating in San Antonio, now that Gladys had removed herself from the picture.

She was from Denver, he wrote, and her name was Mamie Doud, "the girl I run around with since I learned that G.H. cared so terribly for her work."

Years later, Gladys Harding married Cecil Brooks of Abilene. She kept her letters from the young Eisenhower and eventually bound them up. She gave them to her son with instructions that they were not to be opened or published until after her death as well as those of Dwight and Mamie Eisenhower. They are now at the Eisenhower Library.

ABILENE 99-98% PURE SAND SPRINGS WAT...

Gladys Harding

"Apollo Concert Co.

-1915.-

Permanent address:
Abilene, Kansas

PERSONAL

My name is Gladys Harding.

My address is Abilene, Kansas.
U. S. A.

In case of accident, please notify

Mr. Jay Harding

Abilene, Kansas.

The No. of my watch case is 652966.

The No. on the works is 9251289.

The No. on my savings bank book is _____

My weight was __#__ and my

Height __#__ Feet __#__ Inches

on _____

Size of my Hat __#__

"   Gloves Six

"   Drawers #

"   Shirt #

"   Undershirt #

"   Hosiery #

"   Collar #

"   Cuffs #

"   Shoes #

My will is __o—o—o—o__

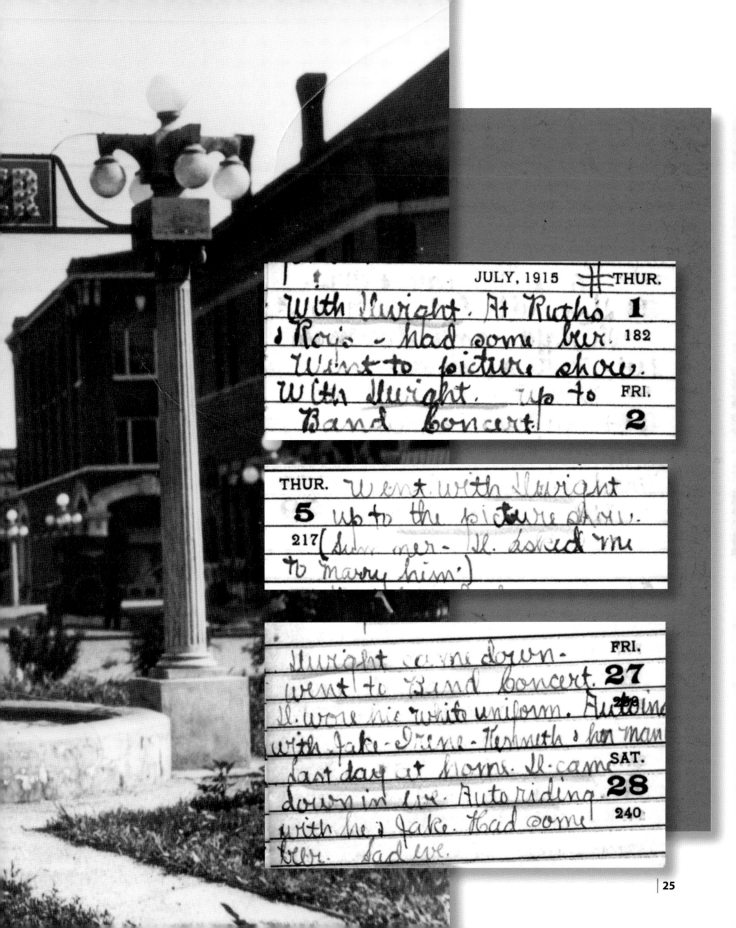

JULY, 1915 # THUR. 1
182

With Dwight. At Ruth's
& Roy's. Had some beer.
Went to picture show.
With Dwight. up to
Band Concert.

FRI. 2

THUR. 5
217

Went with Dwight
up to the picture show.
(Summer - He asked me
to marry him.)

FRI. 27

Dwight came down.
went to Band Concert.
He wore his white uniform. Automo-
with Jake - Irene - Kenneth & her man
last day at home. He came
down in eve. Auto riding
with he & Jake. Had some
beer. Sad eve.

SAT. 28
240

25

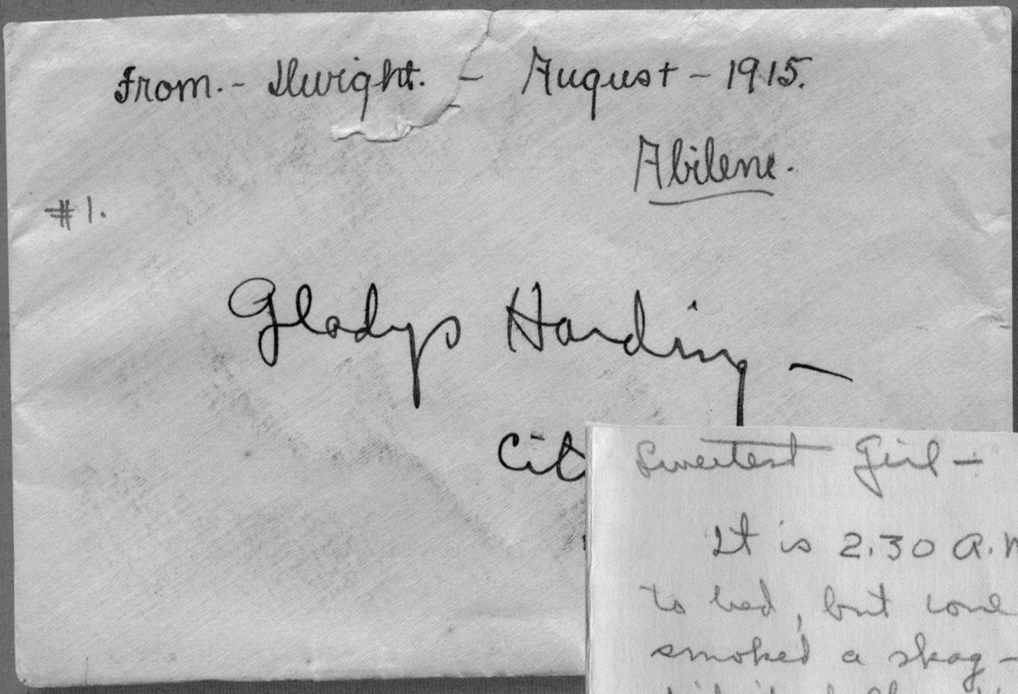

From - Dwight - August - 1915.

Abilene.

#1.

Gladys Harding -

cit...

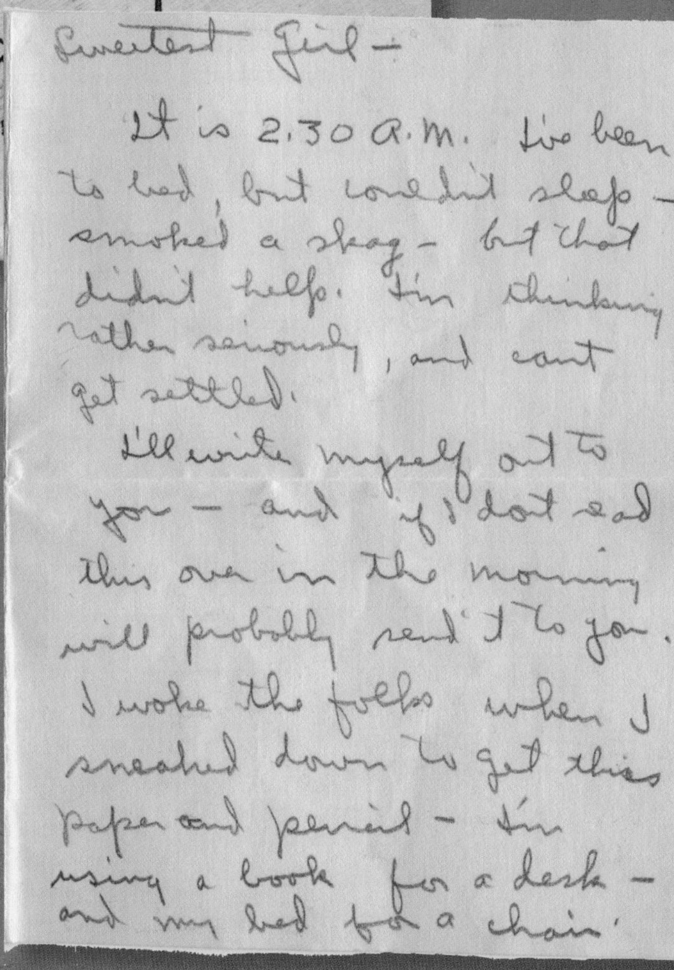

Sweetest girl -

It is 2.30 a.m. I've been
to bed, but couldn't sleep -
smoked a shag - but that
didn't help. I'm thinking
rather seriously, and can't
get settled.

I'll write myself out to
you - and if I don't read
this over in the morning
will probably send it to you.
I woke the folks when I
sneaked down to get this
paper and pencil - I'm
using a book for a desk -
and my bed for a chair.

"...been to bed, but
couldn't sleep...."

If I do send this – please do me this favor – tear it up – Please let it be just a sort of one sided conversation – with you the unwilling listener – and so destroy any all evidence of it.

I think I appreciate you more this eve than ever before. I have a keener realization of your worth and sweetness – and feel how lucky I am that you give me even a thought.

Maybe it's only because I realize that the date of your leaving is drawing so close. that I am thinking so seriously but I believe the real reason is that I am awake to the fact that it was awfully hard for you to say the seven words

this eve

I wanted to hear so badly. And then too, I had not known before how much some of the ones of the past still mean to you.

More than ever, now, I want to hear you say the three words with "better than I ever have anyone in the world"! If ever you can say that to me —— (and if you can you will, because you promised) – then I'll

A profession of love written in the wee hours of the morning, this letter from Dwight Eisenhower was to be read by Gladys Harding and then torn up. She kept it nevertheless. Although the words have been quoted before, the document is reproduced here for the first time.

know that I've won.

From that time — if it ever comes — I'll know you're mine — no matter where you go — or what you do. Whether or not you'll wear my ring would be of small consequence — and such things as promises will be superfluous — I'll know that you'll wait — that nothing can change either you or me — and that someday will make the realization

of my dreams —

For girl I do love you, and want you to know it — to be as certain of it as I am — and to believe in me and trust me as you would your dad.

Please don't think that I'm presuming to be worthy of even the faintest spark of affection from you. I know that I've made miserable mistakes and botches — but girl I'm trying!

It seems so many thoughts crowd to my brain this eve — I'd like to talk to you for hours —

Sept 1st seems so fearfully close tonight, this parting is going to be the hardest so far in my life.

As I sat here smoking I tried

to picture you as you sat in front of your dresser the other night thinking. I know that one thing you thought of was what you told me for the first time.

I don't know how little nor how much you do love me – but I do know that you do not care now like I dare to hope that you will.

As I look back to my home coming this

"Remember sometimes when the train's late and you're sitting in a lonesome station ready to jump to the next dreary town – that your soldier pal loved you...."

summer – and remember my resolution to never let you know that I cared except in a friendly way – I wonder how I ever expected to keep 'it'.

No matter what comes of it, it was inevitable that I should tell you sometime. If you find that nothing can ever come of 'it – you will at least remember sometimes when the train is late, and you're sitting in a lonesome

"But you see dear, I need you so..."

station waiting to jump to the next dreary town — that your soldier pal loved you with the purest, sweetest and strongest love he ever gave to woman, except his mother, and loved you as a man does the one woman, whom in his most cherished dreams, he hopes some day to call his wife.

I've been thinking too of how I told you this evening about jealousy. Girl — I know there no right at all to be jealous, even if there were occasion to be. I also know that jealousy is one of the smallest and meanest traits a fellow can let creep into his nature. But you see dear, I need you so. When I think of Sep. 1, I begrudge every minute I can't see you until then. I keep telling myself that you have other friends you want to see — and

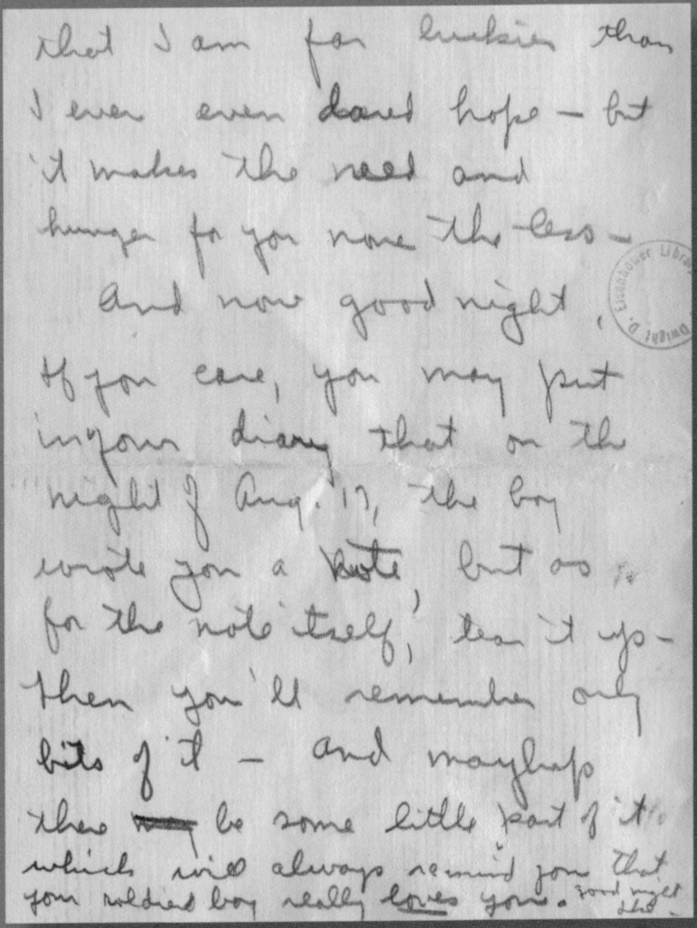

that I am far luckier than
I ever even dared hope — but
it makes the need and
hunger for you none the less —
And now good night.
If you care, you may put
in your diary that on the
night of Aug. 17, the boy
wrote you a note, but as to
for the note itself, tear it up —
then you'll remember only
bits of it — and mayhap
there will be some little part of it
which will always remind you that
your soldier boy really loves you. good night
Ike

"Good night. Ike"

Upon graduating from West Point in 1915, Eisenhower applied for duty in the Philippines. Instead, he was assigned to Fort Sam Houston in San Antonio. It turned out lucky for him.

One Sunday in October, while making the rounds as officer of the day, he was called over to a small gathering. Visiting the wife of another officer was the Doud family of Denver, which often spent winters in San Antonio. Among them was 19-year-old Mamie Geneva Doud. She was "a vivacious and attractive girl, smaller than average, saucy in the look about her face and in her whole attitude," Eisenhower recalled years later in his memoir, *At Ease*. He was "intrigued by her appearance."

For her part, Mamie was taken by the young lieutenant from Kansas. He was different, she once said, from the boys of Denver society – "lounge lizards with patent-leather hair."

Eventually, Eisenhower asked Mamie out. She was making her society debut and her calendar was full, but he persisted in calling the house. Even when he knew she was out, he dropped in on her parents.

In a letter to friend Ruby Norman, Eisenhower attempted a casual tone: "The girl I run around

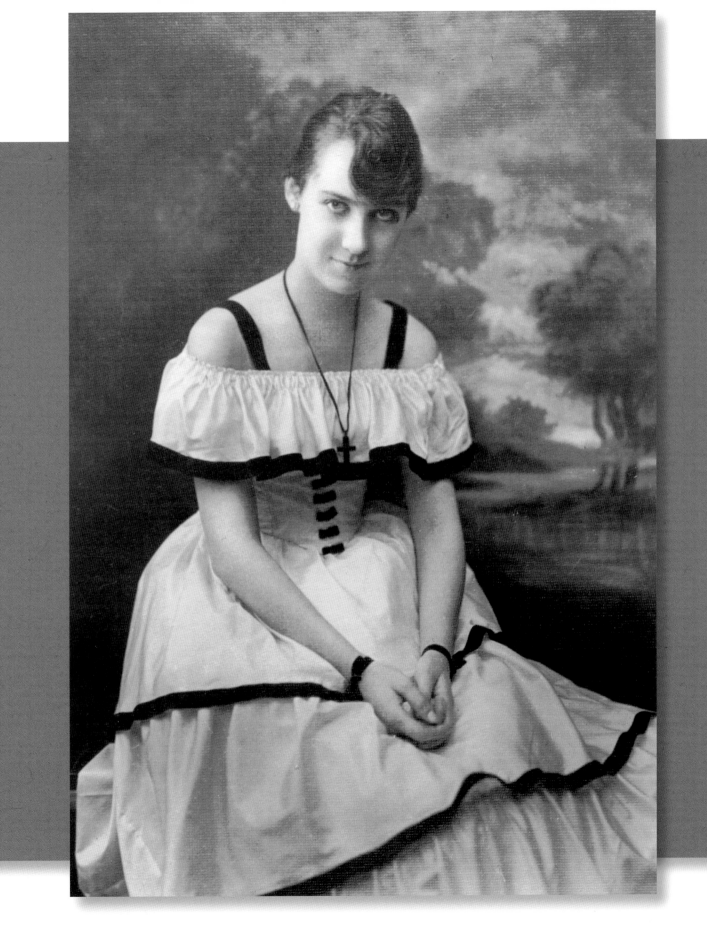

with is named Miss Doud, from Denver. Winters here. Pretty nice – but awful strong for society – which often bores me. But we get along well together and I am at her house when I am off duty – whether it's morning – noon – night." That Christmas, Eisenhower presented Mamie a sterling silver jewelry box. Engraved with her initials, it could not be returned.

Envelope:

After 10 days, return to

Lt. D. Eisenhower 19° Inf.
FORT SAM HOUSTON, TEXAS.

1-30

Miss Ruby Norman,
Sabina,

Gen. Delivery
% American Girls Co.

Letter:

Dearest Ruby:

'Tis a long long time since I've written you, n'est-ce pas? I've really started several times – but 'always something happens – and I get side tracked. It's 10 o'clock now – I'm on guard – and sitting down here in the guard house –

I scarcely ever write a letter any more. Yes – I reckon you'll say – "well what's the trouble" – but there isn't so much. One reason is this "you can't always hold what you have" – My life here, is, in the main uninteresting – Nothing much doing – and I get tired of the same old grind some times.

The girl I run around with is named Miss Doud, from Denver. Winters here. Pretty nice – but awful strong for society – which often bores me.

sent me a fine smoking jacket for Christmas. Mighty nice of her, I thought.

I coached a football team for a little school here this fall. They gave a dance not long ago

at a big hotel, and I attended. When I entered the ball room everybody stopped and started clapping and cheering. I blushed like a baby — Gee! surely was embarrassed.

I made a run for a corner, believe me.

Well girl — write to me — I'll try to do better on writing hereof and sometime — if you're interested I'll tell you all about the girl run around with since I learned that G.H. cared so terribly for her work —

Good night —
as ever
Dwight.

Mamie Doud married Dwight Eisenhower on July 1, 1916, in Denver. In September 1917, Mamie bore a child. He was christened Doud Dwight Eisenhower. Mamie immediately nicknamed him "Little Ike." That soon became "Ikey," and then "Icky."

Mr. and Mrs. John Sheldon Doud

announce the marriage of their daughter

Mamie Geneva

to

Mr. Dwight D. Eisenhower
Lieutenant, United States Army

on Saturday, July the first

Nineteen hundred and sixteen

Denver, Colorado

Doud Eisenhower's porcelain baby cup.

ARMY LIFE

From 1915 through 1922, Dwight Eisenhower:

- Met and married Mamie Geneva Doud of Denver.

- Hitched along on a 1919 Army convoy across the United States, an epic voyage that showed the need for a system of national highways.

- Mastered the training and organizing of troops, and won recognition from superiors for his skill.

Why, then, was Eisenhower disappointed and frustrated in this period of his life?

His principal professional aspiration, to serve in combat, was denied him. Despite his repeated attempts to be sent overseas in World War I, Eisenhower had proven so proficient at training troops that higher officers decided he was more valuable stateside.

His career sometimes seemed jinxed. Once, doing his best to outfit troops, he ordered a particular kind of carrier for entrenching shovels. He was elated when the items arrived – and deflated when they turned out to be the wrong kind. Eisenhower sent them back to the War Department, only to be billed $22.04 for their apparent disappearance. Despite written testimony in support from his colleagues, Eisenhower ultimately had to pay the $22.04. Then he was billed again for the same amount.

Mamie pasted the cancelled check into the family checkbook as a monument to the occasional frustrations of Army life.

The episode, Eisenhower wrote, was more "humiliating than costly" yet he believed that "in that nebulous region called the War Department, I had been found wanting."

Instead of being assigned to France in World War I, he wound

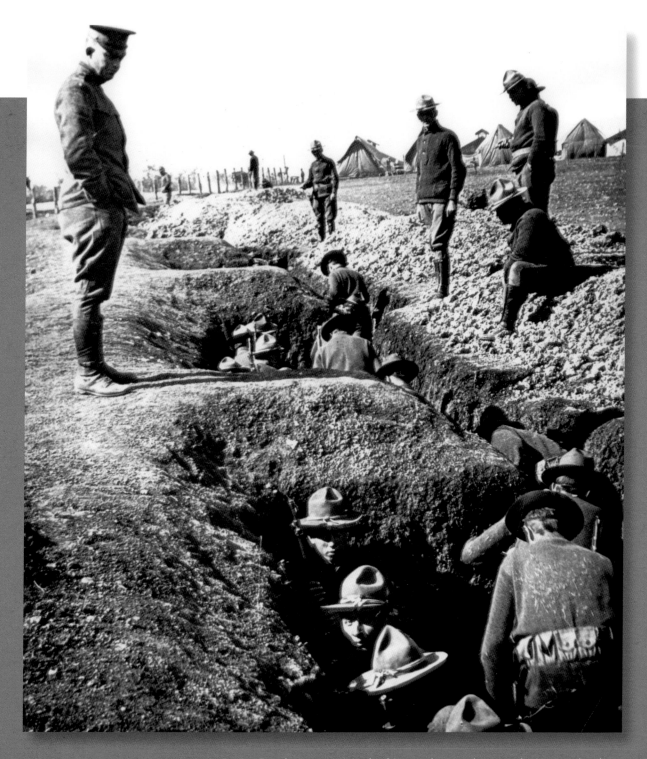

In 1916 Eisenhower supervised as his men dug trenches near the Mexican border.

up in Georgia, where he instructed officer candidates in trench warfare. Then he was sent to Fort Leavenworth, where for several months he instructed provisional second lieutenants. One of them was F. Scott Fitzgerald, who would later win fame as a Jazz Age author.

In March 1918 he was transferred to Camp Meade, Maryland, where he believed he would be commanding a tank battalion headed for Europe. A superior officer, citing his "organizational ability," kept him home.

"I seemed embedded in the monotony and unsought safety of the Zone of the Interior," Eisenhower recalled.

From there he went to Camp Colt at Gettysburg, Pennsylvania, where he supervised training for the newly formed Tank Corps. Then the war ended.

In 1919 Eisenhower became acquainted with George S. Patton Jr. Together for a year, they discussed tank theory, and Eisenhower placed an article extolling the weapon in a military journal. For his effort, he was reprimanded and told to keep his ideas to himself. His schemes did not square with the accepted doctrine of the day.

It would take a while for things to look up for Dwight D. Eisenhower.

Eisenhower as tank commander: a whiz at organizing.

MOTOR TRANSPORT CONVOY COAST TO COAST

TRANSCONTINEN[

★ ★

BETWEEN THE WARS

Road trip. In 1919 it was called the First Transcontinental Convoy and Dwight Eisenhower signed on, he said, as a lark. The task: Move 81 motorized Army vehicles and about 300 men from Washington to San Francisco, more than 3,000 miles.

"To those who have known only concrete and macadam highways of gentle grades and engineered curves, such a trip seems humdrum," Eisenhower wrote years later, when the country boasted a vast network of highways. "In those days, we were not

MOTOR TRANSPORT CONVOY – JULY 7th 1919

© Weller Studio Inc
Balto, Md.
Park Bank Bldg

Because his orders had not come through, Eisenhower wasn't around when the convoy participants lined up for this first-day photo. He joined the next day.

sure it could be accomplished. Nothing of the sort had ever been attempted."

Much of the trip went over dirt roads and mountain trails.

Accounts of the convoy will make any parent who's been on a motoring vacation smile.

It was summer. And the trip took forever, even in 1919 terms.

"In an early span of three days, we spent 29 hours on the road and moved 165 miles," Eisenhower wrote. "This was an average hourly speed of five and two-thirds miles."

There were discipline problems. Vehicles broke down or ran off the road.

Yet there was a genuine military objective: to test various vehicles and determine the difficulty of moving an army across the country.

An element of show business was present as well. The convoy passed through more than 300 communities and usually its arrival was an event. A cartoon caricature of the adventure suggested that locals even watched the soldiers shave. Many of the people along the way may have felt vindicated; several communities and states visited by the convoy already had passed large bond issues for road construction.

The convoy arrived in San Francisco in 62 days, only five days behind schedule. But the wheels kept turning, especially in Eisenhower's own imagination, and continued to turn after he saw the autobahns of Germany in World War II.

"The old convoy had started me thinking about good, two-lane highways, but Germany had made me see the wisdom of broader ribbons across the land," he once wrote.

The impact on the United States four decades later would be profound.

Hobnobbing en route: In Ohio, the officers met with representatives of a company that was intensely interested in highway travel – the Firestones of tire-making fame. Eisenhower posed for a snapshot at the Firestone homestead in Columbiana, Ohio, with William Stuhler, left, and Paul Robinson, second from right. Between them was fellow officer Serano Brett.

Brett & J.

East Wyoming.

One lane, all dirt: The convoy, strung out for a mile along the only road through a desolate stretch of the Mountain west.

"I DIDN'T KNOW WHAT TO DO"

In December 1920 Doud Dwight Eisenhower, the first son of Dwight and Mamie Eisenhower, fell ill. The Eisenhowers were stationed then at Camp Meade, Maryland, and a doctor was summoned from Johns Hopkins medical school in Baltimore.

He diagnosed scarlet fever and placed the child in quarantine, the usual treatment at the time. The illness developed into meningitis. According to an account by Susan Eisenhower, granddaughter of Mamie Eisenhower, Icky died in his father's arms on Jan. 2, 1921. He was 3 years old.

The death devastated the Eisenhowers.

"Within a week he was gone," Eisenhower wrote years later. "I didn't know what to do." He called the child's death "the greatest disappointment and disaster in my life."

"I was on the ragged edge of a breakdown," he wrote a friend.

The Eisenhowers buried Icky in Denver alongside members of Mamie's family. In 1966 Eisenhower had the child's remains disinterred and moved to the chapel on the Eisenhower Library grounds, where eventually and he and his wife would be buried.

Writing in a diary 25 years after his first son's death, Eisenhower mused, "Makes one wonder whether any human ever dares become so wrapped up in another that all happiness and desire to live is determined by the actions, desires – or life – of the second."

Among the family keepsakes was a photo of the child posed humorously at a sign where he should not have been.

JOHN EISENHOWER

Only about 18 months after Dwight and Mamie Eisenhower lost their first child, Mamie gave birth to John Eisenhower in August 1922. Like his father, John would pursue a military career, graduating from West Point, serving in World War II and Korea, and becoming a brigadier general in the Army Reserve. He was also U.S. ambassador to Belgium in the Nixon Administration.

It is as a historian, however, that the younger Eisenhower may be most familiar to the public. He received a graduate degree in English from Columbia University, and his books have included *The Bitter Woods*, a history of the Battle of the Bulge, as well as accounts of the Mexican-American War and Winfield Scott, 19th-century U.S. Army general.

In 2003 John Eisenhower published *General Ike: A Personal Reminiscence*, which detailed his father's relationships with various figures such as Douglas MacArthur, George Patton and George C. Marshall. The book focused on Eisenhower the military officer and not the president because, the younger Eisenhower wrote, he was convinced "that Ike's military career was far more important to him personally than his political life."

General Ike contains vivid recollections of the future president. In one passage about the 1930s John Eisenhower described his father's behavior while listening to the Army-Navy football game on the radio. Clearly his father's regard for Army football was not calculated for effect.

"When that annual ordeal rolled around, I habitually stretched out on the floor to hear the radio better," John Eisenhower wrote, "and I always looked up in wonderment and fear bordering on terror as Ike paced the floor, roared and cursed with either exultation or frustration."

In an interview upon the 2003 publication of *General Ike*, John Eisenhower recalled the awkwardness of parts of his Army career; after all, he was the boss's son. His graduation from the United States Military Academy at West Point on June 6, 1944 – D-Day – was by coincidence, he said, despite what some later claimed. None of his commanding officers wanted him under their command, he said, because of the harm their careers could suffer if anything unfortunate befell him.

Son John was a teenager in 1937, when this photo was made in Manila, Philippines.

Chuckling for a photographer, Eisenhower, far right, and U.S. Army aviators posed amid biplanes at France Field in the Panama Canal Zone

A MENTOR

In 1922, Dwight Eisenhower traveled to the U.S.-operated Panama Canal Zone to serve as executive officer under Brig. Gen Fox Conner. The experience, he would recall, was a "sort of graduate school in military affairs and the humanities."

Conner had been chief of operations under Gen. John Pershing in World War I and evidently he challenged Eisenhower to think big. Under Conner's supervision, the young officer re-fought various military campaigns on paper. When old Abilene friend Everett "Swede" Hazlett, then commanding a submarine, put in at the Canal Zone in 1923, he found Eisenhower living in quarters that included a second-story screened porch outfitted "with drawing boards and texts" for use in studying strategies of old.

An efficiency report filled out by Conner in 1924 recorded superior marks for Eisenhower in tact, leadership, intelligence, judgment and common sense. Conner helped arranged an

Maj. Gen. Fox Conner

    Cmdg. 1st Corps Area.

    A wonderful officer and leader with a splendid analytical mind. He is as loyal to subordinates as to superiors, and like Simonds, Moseley and others of our finest is quick to give credit to juniors.

appointment to the U.S. Army Command and General Staff College at Fort Leavenworth, where Eisenhower finished first in his class.

The years Eisenhower spent under Conner re-directed his career. In an account of the various officers he had served, written in 1932, Eisenhower described Conner as holding "a place in my affections for many years that no other, not a relative, could obtain."

In World War II, when Gen. George Marshall, U.S. Army chief of staff, made Eisenhower his principal plans and operations officer, he wrote his old mentor, Fox Conner, saying, "I sincerely trust that I will be able to do my duty in accordance with your own high standards."

Above: Eisenhower's informal notes about Fox Conner.

Below: Dress whites were in order on warm days entertaining in the Canal Zone. The woman at left is believed to be Mamie Eisenhower. Her husband is the man at right.

Fox Conner.

EFFICIENCY REPORT.

_7.C._

EISENHOWER, DWIGHT D. (O-3822) Major, 20th Inf. Brig
(Name typed.)   (Serial No.)   (Grade.)   (Org'n.)

Camp and Brig Executive Officer under me.

REPORT   2   months, from   July 1, 1924   to   Aug. 31, 1924
Camp Gaillard, C.Z.

E DEFINITIONS, KEEP THEM IN MIND WHEN RATING, AND COMPARE THE
SAME GRADE.
LY POOR performance of duty; EXCEPTIONALLY LACKING in qualification considered.
T performed AS WELL AS SHOULD REASONABLY BE EXPECTED under circum-
stances; not ENTIRELY satisfactory.
AVERAGE: EFFICIENT; duty WELL performed; UP TO STANDARD; qualification SATISFACTORY.
ABOVE AVERAGE: Duty performed MARKEDLY BETTER THAN COULD REASONABLY BE EXPECTED under
circumstances; qualified to MARKED degree.
SUPERIOR: VERY EXCEPTIONALLY EFFICIENT performance of duty; qualified to a VERY EXCEPTIONAL degree.

E. DUTIES HE PERFORMED: (State separately and summarize. Where possible show duration of each in months. Example:
Co. Cmdr. ordinary garrison training, 8 mos. Summary court 6 mos. Brig. Adj. prepared training schedules, Supply Officer.)
In describing the manner of performance of duty, use one of five classifications as given under D amplified as may be appropriate.

Duty.	Months.	Manner of performance.
Camp and Brigade Executive Officer	2	Superior

F. What degree of success has he attained under the following headings: MAKE NO ENTRIES EXCEPT WHERE RATING IS BASED ON PERSONAL OBSERVATION OR OFFICIAL REPORTS DURING PERIOD COVERED BY THIS REPORT. (See par. D above.)

	Inferior.	Below average.	Average (efficient).	Above average.	Superior.
1. Handling men					X
2. Performance of field duties			X		
3. Administrative and executive duties					X
4. As an instructor					
5. Training troops					
6. Tactical handling of troops					

G. Enter on lines below specialties pertaining to any branch of the service as Musketry; Orthopedic Surgery; Motor Transportation; etc. MAKE NO ENTRIES EXCEPT WHERE RATING IS BASED ON PERSONAL OBSERVATION OR OFFICIAL REPORTS DURING PERIOD COVERED BY THIS REPORT. (See par. D above.)

	Inferior.	Below average.	Average.	Above average.	Superior.
1.					
2.					
3.					
4.					
5.					
6.					

H. To what degree has he exhibited the following qualifications? Consider him in comparison with others in his grade and indicate your estimate by marking X in the appropriate rectangle. (See par. D above.)

	Inferior.	Below average.	Average (up to standard).	Above average.	Superior.
1. Physical activity (agility; ability to work rapidly)				X	
2. Physical endurance (capacity for prolonged exertion)					X
3. Military bearing and neatness (dignity of demeanor; neat and smart appearance)					X
4. Attention to duty (the trait of working thoroughly and conscientiously)					X
5. Tact (the faculty of being considerate and sensible in dealing with others)					X
6. Initiative (the trait of beginning needed work or taking appropriate action on his own responsibility in absence of orders)					X
7. Intelligence (the ability to understand readily new ideas or instructions)					X
8. Force (the faculty of carrying out with energy and resolution that which on examination is believed reasonable, right, or duty)					X
9. Judgment and common sense (the ability to think clearly and arrive at logical conclusions)					X
10. Leadership (capacity to direct, control, and influence others in definite lines of action or movement)					X

I. Has he any weaknesses—temperamental, moral, physical, etc.—which adversely affect his efficiency? If yes, describe them. (FACT or OPINION. Line out one.) (See pars. 7 and 9 of instructions.)   NO

Form No. 711, A. G. O.—May 16, 1923.   (PAGE 1.)

In 1923, the United States established the American Battle Monuments Commission. Its first major task was to mark the actions of U.S. troops in France in World War I. In 1927, with the help of his mentor, Fox Conner, Eisenhower was chosen to work for the commission under John J. Pershing, who had commanded American forces in World War I. Eisenhower's job, first in Washington and later in Paris, was to rewrite parts of a guidebook to American battlefields.

Eisenhower took notes in his field journal at a monument on the Meuse River near Sedan, France. Facing page: The book on which he was working.

Copy

THE AMERICAN BATTLE MONUMENTS COMMISSION

State, War, and Navy Building
Washington
August 15, 1927.

Major General Robert H. Allen,
Chief of Infantry,
Washington, D.C.

My dear General Allen:

The detail of Major Dwight D. Eisenhower, who has been assisting the American Battle Monuments Commission in preparing the guide book, expires today. I wish to take this occasion to express my appreciation of the splendid service, which he has rendered since being with us.

In the discharge of his duties, which were most difficult, and which were rendered even more difficult by reason of the short time available for their completion, he has shown superior ability not only in visualizing his work as a whole but in executing its many details in an efficient and timely manner. What he has done was accomplished only by the exercise of unusual intelligence and constant devotion to duty.

With kindest regards, I am

Sincerely yours,

(Signed) *John J. Pershing*
Chairman.

To — my father and mother
Mr. and Mrs. D. J. Eisenhower,
with the love and devotion
of their son,
Dwight.

A GUIDE
TO THE
AMERICAN BATTLE FIELDS
IN EUROPE

PREPARED BY THE
AMERICAN BATTLE MONUMENTS
COMMISSION

Photograph of bearer

Mamie D. Eisenhower

the seal of the Department of State is impressed thereon.

Description of Bearer

Height ___5___ feet ___4___ inches.

Hair ___Brown___

Eyes ___Blue___

Distinguishing marks or features:

Place of birth ___Boone, Iowa___

Date of birth ___Nov 14, 1896.___

_____

Signature of bearer.

4   S   5

The Eisenhower family passports for their journey to Europe. Son John posed for a passport photo with his mother.

Photograph of bearer

passport is issued, In witness whereof the seal of the Department of State is impressed thereon.

4

Description of Bearer

Height 5 feet 10 inches.
Hair light-
Eyes blue

Distinguishing marks or features:

Place of birth Tyler, Texas
Date of birth Oct 14. 1890.

D.D. Eisenhower
Signature of bearer.

S   5

THE BONUS MARCH

In May and June 1932, thousands of World War I veterans descended on Washington, demanding early payment of their service bonus.

A grateful Congress had approved the money eight years before, but for many veterans, it was to come in the form of certificates not scheduled to mature until 1945. In the grip of the Depression, many veterans wanted their money sooner.

For several weeks they camped near the Capitol, rallying support around the country for passage of a bonus bill. In late July, President Herbert Hoover ordered vacant shacks in their temporary camp demolished. A scuffle ensued, possibly prompted by agitators, and eventually U.S. Army troops intervened. Some soldiers used tear gas grenades, which may have set fire to one building. Other fires began.

At the scene was Army chief of staff Douglas MacArthur and assisting him was Maj. Dwight Eisenhower, on special additional duty as his military secretary. The dispersal of the veterans, according to the report that Eisenhower helped write, was for "restoring order in certain sections of this city where considerable bodies of persons had successfully defied police authority and were engaged in riotous activity."

The bonus eventually was paid in 1936, but some believe that the tumultuous dispersal of the veterans contributed to the defeat of Hoover by Franklin Roosevelt in November 1932, and also influenced the passage of the G.I. Bill of Rights in 1944.

Facing page: Eisenhower, left, partly obscured by the straw hat on the man in the foreground, discussed with Douglas MacArthur plans for dealing with the bonus marchers. His log referred to the 1932 matter as the "Bonus Incident."

Aug. 10

    As Gen. MacA's aide took part in Bonus Incident of July 28,
a lot of furor has been stirred up but mostly to make political
capital. I wrote the General's report, which is as accurate as
I could make it. I kept a copy, including most of the enclosures.
(See gray backed booklet)

GETTING ON WITH MACARTHUR

"Essentially a romantic figure," Eisenhower described Douglas MacArthur in 1932. "Magnetic and extremely likable."

After becoming a full-time aide to the flamboyant general in the early 1930s, Eisenhower began logging personal notes about leaders he had known. MacArthur, a man of great ego and many facets, got an extensive description.

In those years, the admiration was returned. Eisenhower noted that MacArthur had placed a "letter of recommendation in my record – and has assured me that as long as he stays in the Army I am among the people earmarked for his 'gang.' "

Later, MacArthur and his staff were assigned to advise the government of the Philippines on military affairs, so in 1935 Eisenhower went to Manila. There he served as the general's chief of staff.

"Very appreciative of good work," Eisenhower wrote in his 1932 log. Indeed, in a handwritten note MacArthur complimented his aide on a report he had written, adding "I do not see how it could be improved upon."

Yet Eisenhower, according to his biographers, eventually clashed with MacArthur. After the declaration of war by Great Britain and France upon Germany in September 1939, Eisenhower asked to be released from his duties with the general.

Years later, when MacArthur led troops in the Korean War, Eisenhower watched his old boss lock horns with President Harry Truman. After the Chinese entered the Korean War in late 1950, MacArthur called for an extension of the war into China. That broke with administration policy, and in April 1951, Truman relieved MacArthur of his command.

Eisenhower wrote MacArthur a few weeks later:

"Sometimes I think that we shall never see the end of the persistent efforts of some sensation-seeking columnists to promote the falsehoods that you and I are mortal enemies. Of course, I need not tell you that, through these years, I have truly valued your friendship."

Facing page: Eisenhower's log, originally hand-written, was transcribed by an aide, Kevin McCann.

uglas MacArthur, General, Chief of Staff

Fifty-two years old. Essentially a romantic figure. I
ve done considerable personal work for him, but have seen far
ss of him than of other seniors now in the dept. Very apprecia-
ve of good work, positive in his convictions - a genius at
ving concise and clear instructions. Consideration of the
incipal incidents in his career leads to the conclusion that
s interests are almost exclusively military. He apparently
oids social duties as far as possible -- and does not seek the

limelight except in things connected with the Army and the
W.D. Magnetic and extremely likable. Placed a letter of
commendation on my record - and has assured me that as long
as he stays in the Army I am one of the people earmarked for
his "gang".

In my opinion he has the capacity to undertake successfully
any position in govt. He has a reserved dignity -- but is most
animated in conversation on subjects interesting him. I doubt
that he has any real political ambition -- and in these days of
high powered publicity and propaganda - I do not expect to see
him ever prominently mentioned for office outside the W. D.

Most people that have known Gen. MacA. like and admire
him to a degree. These same people, however, almost without
exception profess themselves to be incapable of understanding
his policies with respect to the Army's commissioned personnel.

The menti
seems to
ion of "f
officers
older and   He is impulsive - able, even brilliant - qu
one thing   of his views and extremely self-confident. It m
him react   too that he has not appointed some of his new Br
of his "m   any delusions as to their abilities. He is too
personal   The answer is that, in his opinion at least, he
he is fol   course representing the lesser of two evils.

His head shaved in an attempt to defeat the heat of the Philippines, Eisenhower stood by at headquarters as MacArthur spoke on the telephone. The aide's work won high praise, facing page.

COMMONWEALTH OF THE PHILIPPINES
OFFICE OF THE MILITARY ADVISER
1 CALLE VICTORIA
MANILA

congrats
Philippines
✓

Ike —

This is Excellent in every respect. I do not see how it could be improved upon. It accomplishes the purpose in language so simple and direct as to preclude confusion and is flexible enough for complete administration along both lines. — MacA

EFFICIENCY REPORT

(SEE AR 600-185)

...RITER IF POSSIBLE
...NT PROPER NAMES)

...CER REPORTED UPON: .... EISENHOWER, DWIGHT D. ..... 0-3822 ...... Major, Infantry (DOL)
..... (Name) ..... (Serial) ..... (Grade) ..... (Organization)

official status with respect to you ...... On duty in Office of the Chief of Staff. ......

...IOD COVERED BY THIS REPORT ...... 12 ...... months, from ...... July 1, 1934 ...... to ...... June 30, 1935:

...TIONS HE SERVED AT ...... Washington, D. C. ......

...TIONS, KEEP THEM IN MIND WHEN RATING, AND COMPARE THE
...NSIDER CAREFULLY THESE DEFINITIONS,
...FFICER WITH OTHERS IN SAME GRADE.

INFERIOR: EXCEPTIONALLY POOR performance of duty; EXCEPTIONALLY LACKING in qualification considered.

UNSATISFACTORY: Duty NOT performed AS WELL AS SHOULD REASONABLY BE EXPECTED under circumstances;
not ENTIRELY satisfactory.

SATISFACTORY: EFFICIENT; duty WELL performed; UP TO STANDARD; qualification SATISFACTORY.

EXCELLENT: Duty performed in a HIGHLY EFFICIENT manner; qualification BETTER THAN usually accepted as
SATISFACTORY.

SUPERIOR: PREEMINENTLY EFFICIENT performance of duty; qualified to a PREEMINENT degree.

...UTIES HE PERFORMED: (State separately and summarize. Where possible show duration of each in months. Example:
Co. Comdr. ordinary garrison training, 8 mos. Summary court, 6 mos. Brig. Adj. prepared training schedules, Supply Officer.)
In describing the manner of performance of duty, use one of five classifications as given under D, amplified as may be appropriate.

Duty	Months	Manner of performance
	12	Superior
On duty in Office of the Chief of Staff.		

...What degree of success has he attained
under the following headings:
MAKE NO ENTRIES EXCEPT
WHERE RATING IS BASED ON
PERSONAL OBSERVATION OR
OFFICIAL REPORTS DURING
PERIOD COVERED BY THIS
REPORT. (See par. D above.)

G. Enter on lines below any outstanding specialties of value in
the military service. MAKE NO ENTRIES EXCEPT
WHERE STATEMENT IS BASED ON PERSONAL
OBSERVATION OR OFFICIAL REPORTS DURING
PERIOD COVERED BY THIS REPORT.

	Inferior	Unsatisfactory	Satisfactory	Excellent	Superior
1. Handling officers and men					X
2. Performance of field duties					
3. Administrative and executive duties					
4. As an instructor					
5. Training troops					
6. Tactical handling of troops (units appropriate to officers' grade)					

H. To what degree has he exhibited the following qualifications? Consider him in comparison with others in his grade and indicate your estimate by marking X in the appropriate rectangle. (See par.
D above.)

	Inferior	Unsatisfactory	Satisfactory	Excellent	Superior
1. Physical activity (agility; ability to work rapidly)				X	X
2. Physical endurance (capacity for prolonged exertion)				X	X
3. Military bearing and neatness (dignity of demeanor; neat and smart appearance)					X
4. Attention to duty (the trait of working thoroughly and conscientiously)					X
5. Tact (the faculty of being considerate and sensible in dealing with others)					X
6. Initiative (the trait of beginning needed work or taking appropriate action on his own responsibility in absence of orders)					X
7. Intelligence (the ability to understand readily new ideas or instructions)					X
8. Force (the faculty of carrying out with energy and resolution that which on examination is believed reasonable, right, or duty)					X
9. Judgment and common sense (the ability to think clearly and arrive at logical conclusions)					X
10. Leadership (capacity to direct, control, and influence others in definite lines of action or movement)					X

I. Would you *object, *be reluctant, be satisfied, especially desire, to have this officer serve under your command, in peace? In
war? In his present or a higher grade? (Line out inappropriate words. *State reasons.) ...... Yes ......

*object, *be reluctant, ... No ...... If yes, describe

J. Has he any weaknesses—temperamental, moral, physical, etc.—which adversely affect his efficiency?
them. (FACT or OPINION. Line out one.)

In the middle 1930s, MacArthur's report on Eisenhower rated the major as superior in all except two categories. In the early 1950s, Eisenhower assured his former boss that the two of them could get along.

Supreme Headquarters
Allied Powers Europe
15 May 1951

Personal

Dear General:

Sometimes I think that we shall never see the end of the
persistent efforts of some sensation-seeking columnists
to promote the falsehood that you and I are mortal enemies.
Occasionally they go so far as to assert that this antago-
nism existed even before I first met you, when you were
Chief of Staff. I assume their purpose to be an increase
in circulation.

Of course, I need not tell you that, through these years,
I have truly valued your friendship. But I do want to
express my appreciation of the fact that, during all the
stresses and strains to which you have been subjected
since the beginning of World War II, you have never, even
accidentally, uttered a word that could give an atmosphere of plausibility to this curious lie.

The preoccupations of my job are such that it will probably
be months before I can ever find opportunity to return,
even briefly, to the United States. But I must say that
I look forward, as I hope you do, to indulging again on
some quiet evening in the kind of conversation on absorb-
ing military subjects that we had at our most recent
meeting - almost exactly five years ago today, in your
home in Tokyo.

Please convey my warm greetings to Jean, and with best
regard to yourself,

                                        As ever,

                                        The Eisenhower
                                        15 May

General of the Army Douglas MacArthur
Waldorf-Astoria Towers
New York, N. Y.

67

THE GREAT CHALLENGE

On Dec. 7, 1941, Dwight Eisenhower, then assigned to Fort Sam Houston near San Antonio, was taking a nap. An aide woke him with news that Japanese bombers had attacked the Pearl Harbor naval base in the U.S. territory of Hawaii.

"I was absolutely stunned," he recalled.

A week later, Eisenhower was summoned to Washington, where he sat down in the office of George C. Marshall, U.S. Army chief of staff. The Pacific fleet was in ruins. Thousands of American soldiers in the Philippines faced the prospect of a Japanese assault. There was little the United States military establishment could do to help them — at least immediately.

What, Marshall asked Eisenhower, should be our course of

Above: The attack on Pearl Harbor.

Facing page: "Tempers are short!" Eisenhower wrote on a daily calendar meant to surround the face of a clock. He was in Washington in early 1942, trying to figure out something to save American forces in southeast Asia.

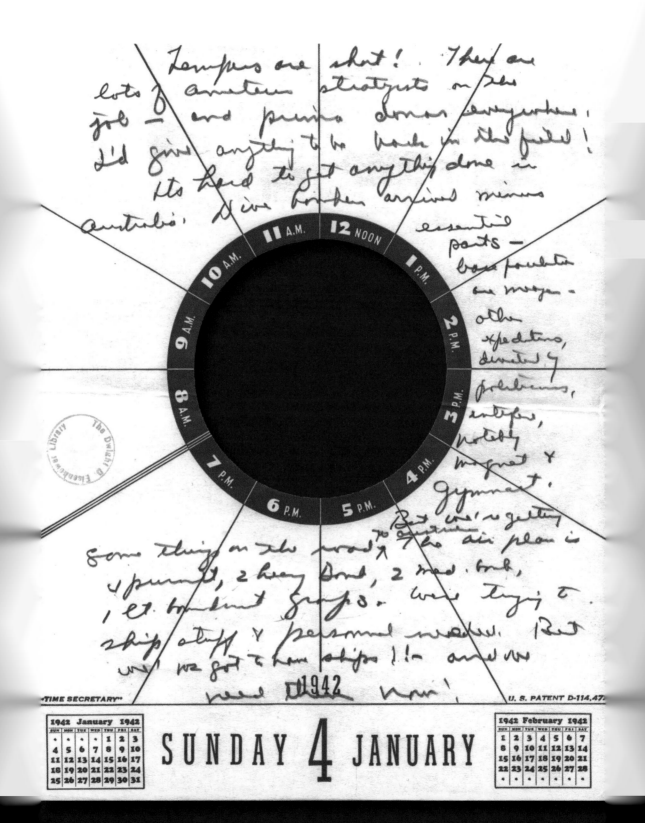

Tempers are short! They are
lots of amateur strategists on the
job — and prima donnas everywhere!
I'd give anything to be back in the field!
Its hard to get anything done in
Australia. Five bombers arrived minus
essential
parts —
base facilities
are meager —
other
expeditions,
delayed by
problems,
entirely,
notably
magnet &
Gymnast.

But we're getting
some things on the road to Australia the air plan is
4 pursuit, 2 heavy bomb, 2 med. bomb,
1 lt. bombard group. We're trying to
ship stuff & personnel westward. But
we got to have ships!! and we
need them now!

"TIME SECRETARY"

U. S. PATENT D-114,47

1942

SUNDAY 4 JANUARY

1942	January				1942	
SUN	MON	TUE	WED	THU	FRI	SAT
·	·	·	·	1	2	3
4	5	6	7	8	9	10
11	12	13	14	15	16	17
18	19	20	21	22	23	24
25	26	27	28	29	30	31

1942	February				1942	
SUN	MON	TUE	WED	THU	FRI	SAT
1	2	3	4	5	6	7
8	9	10	11	12	13	14
15	16	17	18	19	20	21
22	23	24	25	26	27	28
·	·	·	·	·	·	·

action? Eisenhower's response: give him a few hours.

There were few people in the United States whom Marshall could have even asked such a question. For the task, Eisenhower was uniquely qualified. Since his graduation from West Point some 25 years before, he had received a schooling matched by few Americans. Disappointed as he was at not receiving an overseas assignment in World War I, his stateside duties included organizing a tank corps. That was the kind of emergency mobilization, according to historian Carlo D' Este, that Marshall knew he needed.

Also, Eisenhower's service under Gen. Fox Conner in Panama in the early 1920s had represented a graduate-level curriculum in military history and theory. Serving under Gen.

Douglas MacArthur in the Philippines in the 1930s had given Eisenhower a direct knowledge of the Far East and the United States' interests there.

Near sunset, Eisenhower returned to Marshall with a plan to try to halt the Japanese advance. Marshall was impressed.

In June 1942, after Eisenhower arrived home from a trip to England, Marshall told him he was the man who would coordinate U.S. forces in England, and organize the invasion of North Africa. Eventually, Eisenhower would be named to supervise all that followed.

According to one account, Eisenhower told Mamie about it over dinner:

"I'm going to command the whole shebang."

The war came to U.S. territory when Japanese bombers struck Navy warships in Hawaii, crippling the Pacific fleet.

Heading

DW2X V DN3L P BT

WE HAVE ATTACKED FIRED UPON AND DROPPED DEPTH CHARGES ON A SUBMARINE
OPERATING IN DEFENSIVE SEA AREA.

TOD 1724 DEC 7TH

FROM:	ACTION TO:	INFO. TO:
WARD	COM 14	

Release ....   Priority ....   Routine ....   Deferred ....

Div. Comdr.	Capt.	Exec.	Eng.	1st. Lt.	Gun.	Torp.	O.O.D.	Comm.	C'Sary.	Supply	Div. Disb.		

632—S/M Base, PH.—10-13-41—2M.

This telegram recounts what many consider the first shot fired by Americans in the Pacific War in World War II.

While on patrol the morning of Dec. 7, 1941, crew members of the U.S.S. Ward, a newly re-commissioned destroyer from World War I, spotted a small submarine in restricted waters. Commanding the Ward was William Outerbridge, a U.S. Naval Academy graduate who had taken his post on the ship only days before.

About 6:45 a.m. the Ward fired shots from two of its guns and launched depth charges. The submarine – one of five launched by the Japanese on Dec. 6, each carrying a two-man crew and two torpedoes – sank in about 1,200 feet of water. Less than one hour later, Japanese bombers commenced their attack on Pearl Harbor.

In August 1969, a few months after Dwight Eisenhower's death, Outerbridge deposited his papers in the Eisenhower Library. They included the text of the message sent after the submarine sank.

Getting on the same page: Eisenhower skillfully managed competing ideas and clashing egos on both sides of the British-American alliance in World War II. In June 1943, he and George Marshall met with the British in Algiers, above, and heard Winston Churchill lay out proposals. In a sporting moment appropriate to wartime, right, Eisenhower, Churchill and Omar Bradley matched marksmanship.

After Allied forces defeated the Germans in North Africa, it was on to Sicily. There Eisenhower accompanied President Franklin Roosevelt, who named him to oversee the invasion of German-held France. FDR's signed note to inform Stalin of the fact was encased in plastic by the Eisenhower White House and loaned to the Eisenhower Library and Museum by David Eisenhower, grandson of the Allied commander.

CLOSE – BUT THAT CLOSE?

Kay Summersby, Dwight Eisenhower's driver and secretary while he served as Allied commander in Europe, wrote and maintained Eisenhower's desk diaries from 1944 and 1945. Occasionally, Eisenhower made handwritten entries.

She held the diaries for about 30 years and then gave them to Barbara Wyden, an author and ghostwriter, as research material. In 1976, one year after Summersby died, the book *Past Forgetting: My Love Affair With Dwight D. Eisenhower* appeared. The book suggested that Summersby and Eisenhower shared a close and perhaps intimate relationship during the war. In 2001 the Eisenhower Library acquired the diaries from Wyden.

The Library has found no evidence in its archives that a non-professional relationship ever existed.

"The truth of the matter," writes Eisenhower biographer Michael Korda, "is that nobody knows."

Above: Kay Summersby with Telek, one of two Scotties that were pets of the Allied commander. The other, perched at the arms of Eisenhower's chair in Algiers in 1943, right, was named Caacie.

Both outfitted in khaki shirts, Eisenhower and Summersby posed for a snapshot.

Thursday June 1. 1944.

Message from the P.M. Relative...Restrictions on travel and messages should cea se
say D x 7.

Col. Depuis (acting PRO) and Col/ Thor Smith conference with E. Discussed the handling
of press during operations. The C/S and G3 were in a nd out of the office all day.

Friday June 2 1944.

10 a.m. meeting at Southwick House. Portsmouth. Our C.P. is in a wood about a twenty
mintues drive from the above building. We work in trailers which are ver comfortable.
During the da y a message came in from Tommy Thompson saying that the P.M. and F.M.Smuts
also Gen. Ismay will a rrive about 7.15 . in the evening. will stay for about ½ hour.
E. is dining with Monty at '8 p.m.
9. 30. p.m. E. has a conference at Southwick House. Relative weather for D. Day. also
the command organization of our forces in Europe as our army builds up on the continent.

Satunday June 3 . 44

Leave the C.P. ea rly monning for SHAEF 9(Bushey Park) E. has a comference with Lt. Gen
Simpson. Discussed the organization of the 9th. army and agreed upon priority in
Corps Commanders.   Conferences a;so with Tedder and Spaatz. Rela tive. A protest sub-
mitted b y Monty on xskxxgxsxx changes on Air Pla n for the afternoon of D.Da y.
We lea ve Bushey Park ea rly afternoon for our C/P.
E. attends comference at Southwick House. The weather forecast is bad, E. is very depress
ed. However there is going to be another comfernece this evening at 9.30. thixx P.M.
7 p.m. The P.M. F.M. Smuts and Mr. Bevan arive at our C/P. The party sta y g or about 1 hour
9. 30 p.m. E. drives over to Southwick House f or confernece. No chacge in the weather.
D. Day will ave to be postponed.

Sunday June 4 1944.

The P.M. and F.Mm.Smuts also Gen de Gaulle are coming to see E. at the C/P at 3. 30 this
afternoon. De Gaulle is very difficult, sees only his own point of view. He has been
of ta rget for D. Day. At 4. 30. p.m. confernce at Southwick House. The weather forecast
is fair. Monty agrres with E. tha t the Target da te should not be delayed if at all
possible. Final confernce tonight at 9.30. Southwick House. It is a very short one, D.D/

GEN. DWIGHT D. EISENHOWER

D Day fixed   last one

Monday, June 5

4.15 a.m. conference - weather fair

Portsmouth 11.30.

E. inspects troops going
aboard ships (British)
he is greeted with
shouts of "good old Ike"

5.30. Press conference

lasted for 1½ hrs.
Correspondents (4) were informed
of d[...]

Kay Summersby's typed log and notes for the days leading up to D-Day. "The P. M." is British Prime Minister Winston Churchill, "E." is Eisenhower.

has now been decided on. E. has listened to all the advice of his commanders, weather

experts etc, he alone is the one to say---we will go. As E. came out of the conference

he told me that the date of D.Day.

Monday June 5 1944.

We leave the C/P early morning and drive to the docks . E. wishes to see the troops

embarking.xxx   All the forces that E. sees are British, the American troops are not

leaving from Portsmouth. Everywhere E. goes he is greeted with shouts of "Good old Ike"

In the afternoon there is a press conference at the C/P. The correspondents are informed

of D. Day. 6. 30. p.m. E. leaves Portsmouth to visit troops in the Newbury area.

101 Div. (Gen Taylor) E. drives to three airfields to watch the men getting ready to

board the ships. The stars on the car are covered, no one has any idea that the S. C.

is coming to wish them God speed. When he was recognised, the shouts that went up were

tremendous.Gen. Taylor was about the last person to get aboard his ship. E. walked with

him to the door of the C 47. By this time it was getting quite dark, we returned to

101. HQ. with several members of tye staff. had some coffee and then proceeded to climb

on the roof of the building to watch the aircraft circling over the field getting into

formation. It was one of the most impressive sights that anyone could wish to see,

visibility was ferfect, all the stars were gleaming. E. stayed for about ½ hour. We then

started the drive back to our C/P, getting back about 12 /45 a.m.

THE ULTIMATE DECISION

In Dwight Eisenhower's long military career, D-Day marked the principal event.

Against German defenses along the coast of France, the Allies prepared to send almost 133,000 troops from England, Canada and the United States, and about 7,000 ships and landing craft.

Historians can find a rich mine of D-Day photographs and documents at the Eisenhower Library, detailing planning meetings, minute-by-minute accounts of the action on shore and Eisenhower's own actions.

Once he gave the order to go in the early hours of June 5, there was little more for him to do. So that afternoon and evening he visited both British and American troops, describing their demeanor in a cable to General Marshall.

"The enthusiasm, toughness and obvious fitness of every single man were high," he wrote, "and the light of battle was in their eyes."

As soldiers of the U.S. 101st Airborne prepared to embark across the English Channel – the first wave to land in Normandy – Eisenhower wished them well. The uniform and gear of paratrooper no. 23 above is preserved at the Eisenhower Library and Museum.

"...nothing less than full Victory!"

Eisenhower prepared two messages on the eve of D-Day.

One, written by staff members and then edited by the general, was a one-page "Order of the Day" that could be carried by each soldier or sailor.

"The tide has turned!" the order read. "The free men of the world are marching together to Victory!"

SUPREME HEADQUARTERS
ALLIED EXPEDITIONARY FORCE

Soldiers, Sailors and Airmen of the Allied Expeditionary Force!

You are about to embark upon the Great Crusade, toward which we have striven these many months. The eyes of the world are upon you. The hopes and prayers of liberty-loving people everywhere march with you. In company with our brave Allies and brothers-in-arms on other Fronts, you will bring about the destruction of the German war machine, the elimination of Nazi tyranny over the oppressed peoples of Europe, and security for ourselves in a free world.

Your task will not be an easy one. Your enemy is well trained, well equipped and battle-hardened. He will fight savagely.

But this is the year 1944! Much has happened since the Nazi triumphs of 1940-41. The United Nations have inflicted upon the Germans great defeats, in open battle, man-to-man. Our air offensive has seriously reduced their strength in the air and their capacity to wage war on the ground. Our Home Fronts have given us an overwhelming superiority in weapons and munitions of war, and placed at our disposal great reserves of trained fighting men. The tide has turned! The free men of the world are marching together to Victory!

I have full confidence in your courage, devotion to duty and skill in battle. We will accept nothing less than full Victory!

Good Luck! And let us all beseech the blessing of Almighty God upon this great and noble undertaking.

Dwight Eisenhower

Our landings in the Cherbourg – Havre area have failed to gain a satisfactory foothold and I have withdrawn the troops. (This particular operation) My decision to attack at this time and place was based upon the best information available, The troops, the air and the Navy did all that bravery and devotion to duty could do. If any blame or fault attaches to the attempt it is mine alone.

"Our landings... have failed..."

By himself Eisenhower penciled a less-hopeful pre-invasion message. It was prepared not long after a 4:15 a.m. meeting on June 5, when he gave the go-ahead.

It was to be released if the invasion failed.

According to historian Carlo D'Este, Eisenhower put it in his wallet and forgot about it until he gave it to a colleague in July 1944.

"The troops, the air and the Navy did all that bravery and devotion to duty could do," the note read. "If any blame or fault attaches to the attempt it is mine alone."

JUNE 6, 1944

Dummy paratroopers meant to draw enemy fire were part of the first wave of attack. One is on display at the Eisenhower Library and Museum. Real airborne troops came next along with naval bombardments and then waves of GIs aboard landing ships.

Facing page: Kay Summersby's log recounted how Eisenhower got word of initial success. Despite fierce Geman resistance, the Allies held the Normandy beaches. Casualties among American, British and Canadian troops numbered more than 10,000. Next task after securing the beachhead: On into France.

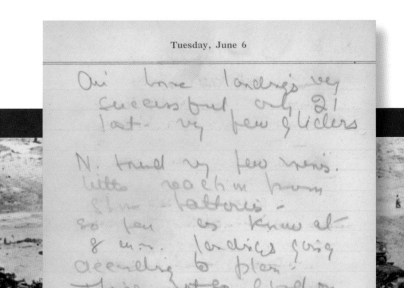

Our own landings very
successful only 21
lost - very few gliders

N. tried very few news.
little reaching from
slow batteries -
so far as known at
8 a.m. landings going
according to plan.
things not so good on
Gen. Gerows beach.
Heavy artillery fire -
unable to land -

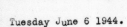

Tuesday June 6 1944.

E. goes to the office which is in a trailer and we all have numerous cups of coffee.

The next few hours are very trying for E., he has done everything in his powere to

ensure success and all he can do now is to wait fro reports to come in.

The first news we had was on the 7 a.a m. BCC news. 8 a.am a report came in to the

effect that the airborne landings were very successful, only 21 nlost. The landings

on thr beaches are going according to schedule, except on gen. Gerows's beach, ve ry

heavy artillery fire making landings inpossible. The rest of the day is spent in

waiting for reports to come in.

LIBERATORS

Flag-waving French hailed the Allied troops marching through Cherbourg, newly freed from German control.

Facing page: A French girl played Betsy Ross, assembling a U.S. flag with needle and thread.

GIs who distinguished themselves, right, won medals from the commander himself.

Four stars, simple fare: The general, jacketed against the chill, stirred his coffee on what was to be a busy day in November 1944 at his advance command post in Gueux, France. British Prime Minister Winston Churchill and his top military commanders would have lunch with Eisenhower that day. Gueux is west of Reims, the city in northeastern France where the Germans would surrender the next spring.

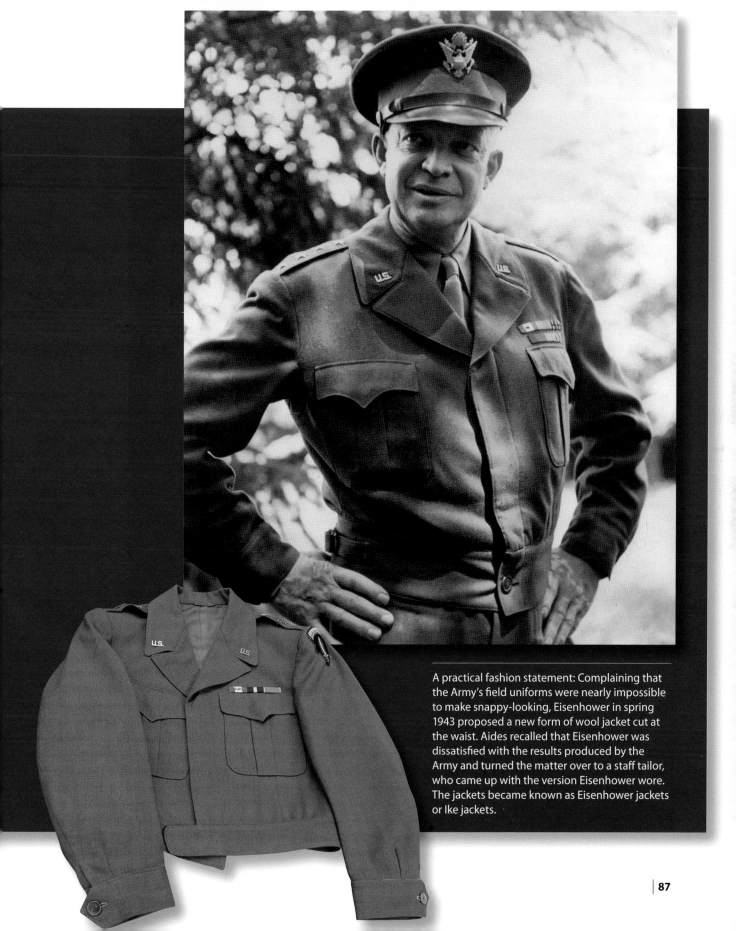

A practical fashion statement: Complaining that the Army's field uniforms were nearly impossible to make snappy-looking, Eisenhower in spring 1943 proposed a new form of wool jacket cut at the waist. Aides recalled that Eisenhower was dissatisfied with the results produced by the Army and turned the matter over to a staff tailor, who came up with the version Eisenhower wore. The jackets became known as Eisenhower jackets or Ike jackets.

Eisenhower spent hours with fellow commanders such as Omar Bradley, left and Ira Wyche in strategy sessions. But he also traveled to greet and encourage the troops, as he did these reinforcements arriving in Le Havre, France, in February 1945, below , and soldiers of the 8th Infantry Division in Belgium, facing page, in late 1944.

FRIDAY APRIL 20Continued.

E. leaves the office about noon to visit Monty at his Tac H.Q.

E. gets back to he office late afternoon. Conference with Gen. Lee re
supply problems.

10 members of Parliament arrive from London. E. meets them in heWar Room
they are going to see some of the consentration caps.

E. is flying to Versaillles this evening to speend   the night with
Bedell.

SATURDAY APRIL 21.

E. arrives back from Versailles 9. 30. Has a long conference with menbers
of his staff. We are expecting to join foces with tye Rssians in he next
few days. E.. keeps on getting messages from the C.C.S's on the subject.
Gen. Lear re theatre matters. Generals Osborne and col PauThompson.
Gen. Spaatz is dining with E. this evening.

SUDAY APRIL 22.

Gen Betts...The usual number of cases. Gen. Littlejohn has just come
back for the U.S. Message from the C'C.S 's. Relative release of news
when the American forces and the Russians join forces. The news must be
released jointly In Washington and London. As usual we don't know what
the Russians are going to do. E. leaves the office early afternoon.

MONDAY APRIL 23.

E. attends war room conference. Everyone is expecting our forces to join
with tye Russians any day. Bedell leaves for N amour to spend he night
Bradley. Gen. Morg an and A.M. Robb spend xiaixx about an hour with E.
discussing the present offensive. We expect the German to surrender
in the near furture.

TUESDAY APRIL 24.

Gen . Lear. Theatre problems. Gen Osbourne. Educational program.
E. writes lettee to gen. Marshall. Two calls from the P.M. in London.

TUESDAY APRIL 24 Continued.

Realtive....The plight of the Dutch population, many of them are starv-
ing. We are doing our best to get hem foof thtough the Red Cross.
E. called Bradley several times during the dy, re our metting the Russian
forces. Bedelll arrives bask frm 12th Army Group. E. has a very heavy
day. He is leaving for Paris his afternoon to visit Gen Wogan who is in
hospital, he was badly wounded several weeks ago. He formly commaned
the 13th Armoured Div.

WEDNESDAY APRIL 25.

E. arrives bask frm Paris. Conference with Bedell, Bull and Clay. A larte
party of members of Congress are arriving here this afternoon to visit
the consentration camps. They came at E.'s invitation. E. meets them in
the war room and afterwards gives them lunch.
Directive from Monty...For once he is in complete acford with E(s views.
Call from the P.M. in the afternoon. A message has reached the P.M. through Switzerland that Hitler has had a complete break down in he last few
days. Himmler now prôses to surrender the Western front. This is not a
military proposal but purely a governmental one.
The Russians have now almost surrounded Berlin and are advancing towards
the cevtre of he city.
THURSDAY APRIL 26.

Long message from he P.M. Relative.. Himmler surrendering the Wester
Front. E. amd the staff are under he belief that his is a last effort on
the part of he German to split he Allies. Chiefly the Russians.
Moscow has been informed, so has Washington.
Message form Gen. Marshall. (1(He has offered t o send Hodges to the
Pacific as soon as the war is over in the West. (2)Bradley was also
offered the chacne of going, bt only as a Army Commnder. Mac Arthur is
not having any Group Commanders in his theatre. E. calls Bradeley and
tells him the score. Naturally Bradley said that he would go anywhre
Gen. Marshall waned him th go, but it was pretty obvious tht he didn't
want to g as a Army Commander. Hodges wasdeligḥted at he prospect of

The log kept by Kay Summersby recounted the Allied advances and the German
failures in April 1945, the final days of the war in Europe.

MISSION FULFILLED

Faced with a moment that called for grand language, Dwight Eisenhower chose understatement.

The German military surrendered on May 7, 1945, in Reims, France, its commanders signing the documents at 2:41 a.m. Eisenhower did not attend the ceremony. After it ended, the German officers were led to his office, where Eisenhower asked whether they understood the terms.

After the Germans left, photographers were admitted to Eisenhower's office, where he smiled and held aloft the two pens that had been used. Next came champagne, but apparently little gaiety.

The last act was to compose a cable to Eisenhower's commanding officers. Staff members groped for phrases appropriate to the occasion. Ultimately Eisenhower rejected them all and wrote his own message.

In a brief celebration, above, the Allied commander flashed the pens used by Lt. Gen. Walter Bedell Smith, left, in the German surrender. Facing page: One of the pens held by the Eisenhower, right, along with the cable announcing victory. The pen is on loan to the Museum from David Eisenhower.

SHAEF FORWARD

STAFF MESSAGE CONTROL

OUTGOING MESSAGE

~~TOP SECRET~~

U R G E N T

TO	: AGWAR FOR COMBINED CHIEFS OF STAFF,
	AMSSO FOR BRITISH CHIEFS OF STAFF
FROM	: SHAEF FORWARD, SIGNED EISENHOWER
REF NO	: FWD-20798 TOO: 070325B

SCAF 355

    The mission of this Allied Force was
fulfilled at 0241, local time, May 7th, 1945.

                    EISENHOWER.

ORIGINATOR   : SUPREME COMMANDER   AUTHENTICATION: J B MOORE,
                                        Lt Colonel

INFORMATION   : TO ALL GENERAL AND SPECIAL STAFF DIVISIONS

SGS Dist	COPY No.
Sc	1/2
DSC	3
CS	
DCS	
CAO	
DCS AIR	
SGS	4
COOR	5
M	6
	7
	8/9
Mr	10

FS OUT 3674   7 MAY 1945   0324B   JOB/jg   REF NO: FWD-20798
                                                  TOO: 070325B
                                                  COPY NO.

"INDESCRIBABLE HORROR"

In mid-April 1945, generals Eisenhower, Omar Bradley and George Patton visited the Nazi concentration camp at Ohrdruf-Nord. Afterward, Eisenhower aide Mickey McKeough described his boss this way:

"Sick…and very angry."

Eisenhower's outrage turned to resolve to tell the world about the camps.

On April 19, he suggested to U.S. Army Chief of Staff George Marshall that up to 12 members of Congress, as well as a similar group of prominent editors, make a trip to see the camps. Marshall's reply, sent the next day, confirmed the idea's approval by President Roosevelt. A similar exchange with British Prime Minister Winston Churchill occurred a few days later.

Subsequent news accounts of the camps prompted a question at a press conference at the Pentagon in June about Eisenhower's role in the publicity and whether he found it useful.

"I think I was largely responsible for it," Eisenhower said, "so I must have thought it was useful."

It was almost impossible to adequately describe what he saw, Eisenhower said.

"I think people ought to know such things," he said. "I think the people at home ought to know what they are fighting for and the kind of person they are fighting against."

Writing to Marshall on April 15, Eisenhower said that Patton had refused to follow him into a certain room.

"I made the visit deliberately," Eisenhower wrote Marshall, "in order to be in a position to give first-hand evidence of these things if ever, in the future, there develops a tendency to charge these allegations merely to "propagandize."

Facing page: Accompanied by survivors dressed in their striped uniforms, Eisenhower toured a Nazi concentration camp in Gotha, Germany, where former prisoners described the scenes. The result was this cable to his boss, George Marshall.

SHAEF MESSAGE FORM

CALL	CIRCUIT No.	PRIORITY	TRANSMISSION INSTRUCTIONS
	NR 21		

SPACES WITHIN HEAVY LINES FOR SIGNALS USE ONLY

FROM (A)	SHAEF FWD	ORIGINATOR Supreme Commander	DDE/nmr	DATE-TIME OF ORIGIN 19 April 1945

TO FOR ACTION   AGWAR   191215 B.

TO (W) FOR INFORMATION (INFO) ~~SECRET~~   EYES ONLY   MESSAGE INSTRUCTIONS   GR 106

(REF NO.) FWD19461.   (CLASSIFICATION) ~~SECRET~~ EYES ONLY

WE CONTINUE TO UNCOVER GERMAN CONCENTRATION CAMPS FOR POLITICAL PRISONERS IN WHICH
CONDITIONS OF INDESCRIBABLE HORROR PREVAIL.   FROM EISENHOWER TO GENERAL MARSHALL
FOR EYES ONLY.   I HAVE VISITED ONE OF THESE MYSELF AND I ASSURE YOU THAT WHATEVER
HAS BEEN PRINTED ON THEM TO DATE HAS BEEN UNDERSTATEMENT. IF YOU WOULD SEE ANY
ADVANTAGE IN ASKING ABOUT A DOZEN LEADERS OF CONGRESS AND A DOZEN PROMINENT EDITORS
TO MAKE A SHORT VISIT TO THIS THEATER IN A COUPLE OF C-54s, I WILL ARRANGE TO HAVE
THEM CONDUCTED TO ONE OF THESE PLACES WHERE THE EVIDENCE OF BESTIALITY AND CRUELTY
IS SO OVERPOWERING AS TO LEAVE NO DOUBT IN THEIR MINDS ABOUT THE NORMAL PRACTICES
OF THE GERMANS IN THESE CAMPS.   I AM HOPEFUL THAT SOME BRITISH INDIVIDUALS IN
SIMILAR CATEGORIES WILL VISIT THE NORTHERN AREA TO WITNESS SIMILAR EVIDENCE OF
ATROCITY.

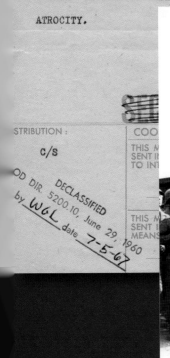

DISTRIBUTION :

c/s

DECLASSIFIED
OD DIR. 5200.10, June 29, 1960
by WGL date 7-5-67

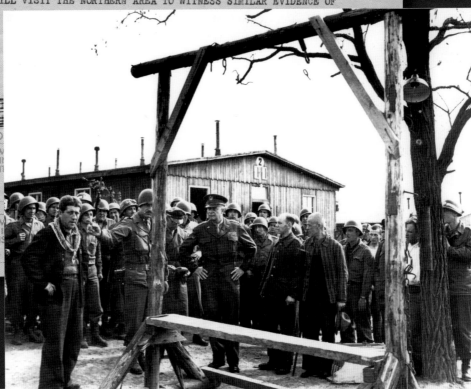

A concentration camp roster retrieved by Allied forces.

Facing page: One GI used official SS stationery to write home about what troops discovered.

Waffen-ϟϟ
ϟϟ-Standortkommandantur
Dachau

Dachau 3, den
Fernruf Dachau 293

Betreff:
Bezug:
Anlagen:

May 11, '45.

of seeing as many as 500,000 men killed at another camp, and of seeing children of the Polish girls (mistresses for ϟϟ troops) dashed to death before their mother's eyes. The recent arrivals here are those that were forced to march from other camps before the onrushing American armies. One fellow told me that of 6000 who started from Friedberg, less than 2500 got here; the others being killed on the way.

A Frenchman I talked with is here along with every other male inhabitant of his village because someone in that village enlisted as English paratrooper before the invasion.

Ten thousand Americans are supposed to have been here, but when we came too close they were pulled out to Munich in hope that their presence there would prevent us from bombing and shelling the city. It didn't.

The most amazing thing to me is that other camps could be worse. But the prisoners stress that this is a "concentration" camp, and that the elimination camps are, by far, worse in every respect.

More tomorrow,

Love,

Harold.

As Army chief of staff after World War II, Eisenhower attracted crowds. In 1947 autograph-seekers surrounded him at the Fairbanks Golf and Country Club on his tour of U.S. bases in Alaska. In the latter part of the decade, he was named president of Columbia University in New York.

BETWEEN BIG JOBS

The first time anyone mentioned the possibility of becoming president to Dwight Eisenhower, it was 1943 and Allied forces – triumphant in North Africa – had landed in Italy. A war correspondent reminded him how Americans traditionally considered successful generals of large armies presidential material – as with George Washington or Andrew Jackson.

Eisenhower told the reporter that he'd been out in the sun too long.

Nevertheless, both Republicans and Democrats were eager to claim him. While riding through the conquered streets of Berlin in 1945 with President Truman, Eisenhower was startled to hear Truman offer him anything he wanted – including the White House in 1948. Eisenhower begged off, but Truman kept trying, even offering to become Eisenhower's running mate. A 1947 diary discovered in recent years at the Truman Library in Independence documented that scenario.

Eisenhower spent the early postwar years in Washington as U.S. Army chief of staff. One of his priorities was the unification of the country's land, sea and air forces, allowing them to respond to threats in a more coherent fashion.

In 1948, he became president of Columbia University in New York. Meanwhile, he demonstrated his continuing interest in public policy by founding the American Assembly, a non-partisan public affairs forum.

In 1950, Truman asked Eisenhower to become the head of the North Atlantic Treaty Organization. As NATO's first commander, it was his task to forge a new alliance from a group of European powers more used to being enemies than allies.

As usual, Eisenhower's plate was full.

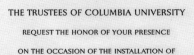

THE TRUSTEES OF COLUMBIA UNIVERSITY

REQUEST THE HONOR OF YOUR PRESENCE

ON THE OCCASION OF THE INSTALLATION OF

DWIGHT DAVID EISENHOWER

AS THIRTEENTH PRESIDENT OF COLUMBIA UNIVERSITY

ON TUESDAY, THE TWELFTH OF OCTOBER

ONE THOUSAND NINE HUNDRED AND FORTY-EIGHT

AT TWO O'CLOCK IN THE AFTERNOON

PLEASE REPLY BEFORE
SEPTEMBER FIFTEENTH TO
THE SECRETARY OF THE UNIVERSITY

CARDS OF ADMISSION
WILL BE REQUIRED AND
WILL BE MAILED ON
RECEIPT OF ACCEPTANCE

FOOTBALL: A LIFELONG CALL

Love of football, in part, led Dwight Eisenhower to West Point and his career in the U.S. Army.

He had played the game at Abilene High and told a friend he wanted to attend the University of Michigan, which fielded one of the best college football teams in the country. The friend urged Eisenhower to seek an appointment to a service academy. Perhaps he could play for Navy.

Instead, Eisenhower qualified for West Point. His second year at the Military Academy he played on the varsity football team. He was listed at 5 feet 11 inches tall and 180 pounds. After a victory against Rutgers, *The New York Times* declared Eisenhower "one of the most promising backs in Eastern football…."

That season, against Carlisle College, he played against the legendary Jim Thorpe. In Army's next game, against Tufts, Eisenhower injured his knee. Doctors told him that the damage would end his football career. After that, he once recalled, life "seemed to have little meaning…."

He consoled himself by assisting the Army coaching staff. In fall 1913, Eisenhower wrote his Abilene friend Ruby Norman, urging her to root for Army against Navy ("…you had better, if you don't want your head pounded off…") and thoughtfully recorded the 1913 Army results to that point – in case she had not kept up with the Cadets' season.

In that list was Army's one loss – 35-13 to Notre Dame. As it turned out, that game was a tipping point in college football history. Notre Dame – then considered

At West Point, Eisenhower ran the ball and punted it, too. After injuring his knee, he resigned himself to building support for the Army team.

We beat a little team yesterday 14-7. We used quite a bunch of subs. Our total now is

Army 29 — Stevens 0
" 34 — Rutgers 0
" 7 Colgate 6
" 2 Tufts 0
" 77 Albright 0
" 55 Villa nova 0
" 14 Springfield 9
" 13 Notre Dame 35

231 — 48

It wouldn't look bad except for the Notre Dame game — we were surely going badly that day.

Its time to go to chapel — so I must ease along my way — Remember that it is good to write once in a while, just to keep in practice, — also that West Point, N.Y. looks awfully nice as an address on an envelope.

good bye for now
yours
Dwight.

Eisenhower's West Point letter sweater lasted him through a coaching assignment at Camp Meade in 1920 and is preserved today at the Eisenhower Library and Museum, along with a Military Academy pennant. In a letter to Abilene friend Ruby Norman, above left, he described the Army football season and provided the scores of each game.

Beside General George Patton, Eisenhower took in a postwar intramural football game in Nuremberg in October 1945.

a small Indiana school of little importance in the football universe – filled a last-minute spot on the Army schedule after Yale University backed out.

One member of that Notre Dame team was Knute Rockne, who had spent the summer with quarterback Gus Dorais experimenting with varieties of the forward pass. In the game against Army, Rockne later recalled, he caught a pass for a touchdown and it became a defining moment in his life. Five years later, Rockne became Notre Dame's coach.

Eisenhower, in his 1913 letter to Ruby Norman, was still hurting.

"It wouldn't look bad except for the Notre Dame game," he wrote. "We were surely going badly that day."

Unable to play, Eisenhower became a cheerleader. That, wrote historian Stephen Ambrose, gave Eisenhower his first experience at public speaking, addressing the entire cadet corps the night before a game. The editors of

the Army yearbook remembered that in the 1915 annual, published upon Eisenhower's graduation:

"At one time he threatened to get interested in life and won his "A" by being the most promising back in Eastern football, but the Tufts game broke his knee and the promise. Now Ike must content himself with tea, tiddledywinks and talk, at all of which he excels."

Yet football remained important to him. As president of Columbia University in the late 1940s, Eisenhower helped persuade Lou Little, the university football coach, not to jump to Yale.

Historians also have noted parallels between generalship on the football field and the battlefield. In private talks with officers in the campaign across western Europe, they noted, Eisenhower filled his speech with gridiron rhetoric such as "hit the line" or "pull an end run."

In his 50s and president of Columbia University, above, Eisenhower attended football practice with Lou Little, whom he persuaded to stay on as coach. Right: Dwight and Mamie attended a game for players 150 pounds and under. The teams: Army and Navy.

26 December 1946

Thank you, General Taylor, for allowing me to take part once again in
a "beat the Navy Football Rally."

Throughout the season the country's sports writers have been exhaust-
ing a vast supply of adjectives in a futile attempt to describe the
excellence of this West Point Team.

Every Army man applauds these sentiments; yet all of us know that on Saturday afternoon the Navy will be out there battling to make a season's
reputation in a single game. The record book will mean nothing to
them except that they will shoot the works in the attempt to take
over your record and so share in its glory. Against Navy desperation
we will pit the best coach and staff and the best team in the land!
Though the Navy will be alert, courageous and skillful they will meet
in every play their superiors in alertness, courage, and in skill.
Behind our team will be every man of the Corps. And behind the Corps
will be every man who now wears or has ever worn the uniform of the
United States Army. Ten million men, and their friends, will follow
every move - will cheer you on and wish you well.

Just a word to co-Captains Davis and Blanchard and you other men of
the squad who, on Saturday, will be playing your final game for West
Point. You have compiled a glorious record of success - yet the feature
of your play that gives me the greatest thrill is the sportsmanship you
have so gallantly and invariably displayed. In the excellence of your
play you have been superb - in your good sportsmanship you have typified
all that's best in the United States Corps of Cadets. I can think of no
xxhxx higher words of praise!

> "The Navy will be out there battling to make a season's reputation in a single game.... [but] they will meet in every play their superiors in alertness, courage, and in skill."

And now- <u>BEAT NAVY</u> - and out of respect for the blood pressure of your older comrades - don't fool around about it! Bring up the guns, the bombers, the fighters, the tanks and the good old infantry - hold back nothing your brains can devise and your hearts sustain! Make it the best game you ever played - team and Corps together - make it your greatest victory, one that all of us will remember as long as we may live.

GOOD LUCK!

In December 1946, Eisenhower addressed the Army squad before its annual game with Navy. At the time Army was led by Earl "Red" Blaik, who compiled an 18-year record of 121-33-10 and brought Army its only three national championships in 1944, 1945 and 1946. Eisenhower, two years removed from the Normandy invasion, leaned hard on military metaphors. "BEAT NAVY," he said, "and out of respect for the blood pressure of your older comrades – don't fool around about it!" Army beat Navy, 21 to 18. Eisenhower's blood pressure was not recorded.

A NEW CRUSADE

In September 1951, U.S. Sen. Henry Cabot Lodge Jr. went to see Eisenhower in Europe, where he was head of NATO, and insisted that the general was the Republican Party's only hope in the 1952 election. Four months later, evidently without asking the general, Lodge said he would put Eisenhower's name on the New Hampshire ballot – as a Republican.

In February 1952 aviator Jacqueline Cochran arrived at Eisenhower's home near Paris to show him film of 15,000 of his supporters demonstrating in Madison Square Garden. On George Washington's birthday, 19 members of Congress wrote Eisenhower a letter urging him to run. One was a future president himself, Gerald Ford.

Eisenhower decided to jump in. His first major campaign appearance was in June 1952 in Abilene. For that

Once persuaded to enter the race, Eisenhower was a natural as a candidate, looking every bit the commander out of uniform – and continually flashing his engaging grin.

event Abilene went Hollywood, with spotlights tracing the night sky. A parade included a float featuring several Abilene residents dressed in severe high-button shirts and modest black bonnets, representing the first of the Eisenhower clan to arrive in 1878.

In his speech, Eisenhower's concerns were international, and he warned of the ambitions of the Communist bloc and the futility of isolationism.

"My Abilene visit," he later wrote, "was, for me, the beginning of a new kind of life."

The next month he received the Republican nomination at the party's Chicago convention.

"I know something of the solemn responsibilities of leading a crusade," he told the delegates. "I have led one."

Memorabilia from the 1952 GOP presidential campaign.

EISENHOWER DEMONSTRATION RALLY
BLACKSTONE THEATRE
60 EAST BALBO DRIVE
TUESDAY, JULY 8, 1952 — 10:00 A.M.
ADDITIONAL TICKETS AVAILABLE AT BOX OFFICE
AIR-COOLED
THE ARCUS TICKET CO.
CHICAGO

1952
Republican
National Convention
Chicago, Illinois

MRS. "IKE" EISENHOWER

Mamie Eisenhower received this campaign cooler during
the 1952 Republican National Convention. (53-168.1-2)

I LIKE
IKE

CAN NATIONAL CONVENTION

Only months after being drafted as a candidate, Eisenhower accepted the 1952 GOP nomination for president. His two-armed wave would become a familiar gesture to Americans in the 1950s.

Facing page: After the Republican Convention, Eisenhower spent time in Colorado with his running mate, Richard Nixon. The two had met only twice before. Fly fishing was one of Eisenhower's favorite pastimes and he showed a suitably attired Nixon the ins and outs of casting.

CAMPAIGNING

Some of Eisenhower's admirers considered him above politics, yet in 1952 he dived right into the traditional style of campaigning – especially the campaign train.

He traveled more than 20,000 miles by rail in what probably was the last long-distance traditional whistle-stop presidential campaign, according to Michael Korda in *Ike: An American Hero*. Eisenhower was sufficiently struck by the ritual of train campaigning that he devoted long, often self-deprecating passages to it in his 1963 memoir, *Mandate for Change*.

His wife, Mamie, proved an enormous asset to the campaign. Korda reminds the reader what Eisenhower, in his memoir, had not: Democratic nominee Adlai Stevenson and his wife had divorced in 1949.

In 1952 Eisenhower captured 442 of 531 electoral votes and received just more than 55 percent of the popular vote.

Of all issues in the campaign, wrote historian Stephen Ambrose, the most important reason for Eisenhower's victory was his personal popularity. It was, Ambrose said, "much more his triumph than the Republicans.' "

Above: The last car of Eisenhower's campaign train carried this backlighted sign urging voters to Look Ahead, Neighbor! (by voting for the GOP ticket).

Facing page: Still in robes, the Eisenhowers waved to photographers at an unscheduled train stop in the wee hours of the morning.

THE EISENHOWER ERA

Inauguration Day for Dwight Eisenhower, January 20, 1953, marked "the most hostile transition of the twentieth century," wrote historian Stephen Ambrose. Some of it had to do with protocol.

President Harry Truman had felt insulted when, on the morning of the inauguration, Eisenhower arrived at the White House but did not enter the building – a gesture that Truman believed was required by custom and propriety. Making the morning more awkward was Truman's lingering resentment over Eisenhower's campaign, during which he had criticized the Truman Administration's foreign policy. As commander of the North Atlantic Treaty Organization in Europe, Eisenhower had been a principal partner in that policy, Truman believed. The two men rode together to the Capitol in an icy coolness.

Those moments, however awkward, seemed to be the exception on an otherwise glorious day for the new president and his family. Mamie, indeed, was thought to have contributed substantially to her husband's election.

In her biography of Mamie Eisenhower, granddaughter Susan Eisenhower described a palpable excitement shown by spectators at campaign rallies for Mamie. On inauguration day, Susan Eisenhower continued, the new president seemed to acknowledge his wife's role in his victory when he "spontaneously turned to his First Lady and kissed her for all to see, on this, the most widely covered event that had ever been broadcast on television."

Eisenhower took the oath of office from Chief Justice Fred Vinson as President Harry S. Truman, former President Herbert Hoover and Vice President Richard Nixon looked on. At far left were Eisenhower's wife, Mamie, and son, John.

A GOP RESTORATION

Eisenhower's election represented the Republicans' first return to the White House since Herbert Hoover vacated it 20 years before. The exhilaration of the Republican faithful manifested itself in an inaugural parade so long that even the new president noticed.

"Not until nearly seven o'clock," Eisenhower said, "did the last two elephants go by."

On his first full day in office, Jan. 21, 1953, Eisenhower paused to note the event for posterity. "Plenty of worries and difficult problems," he wrote. "But such has been my portion for a long time."

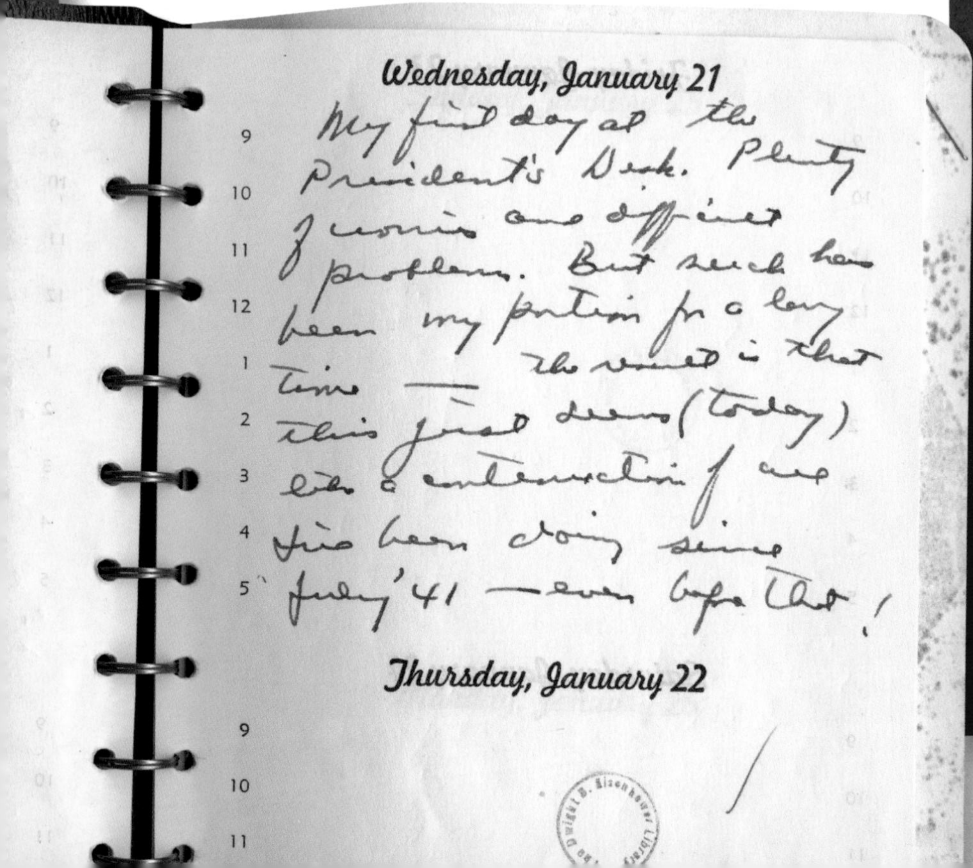

Wednesday, January 21

My first day at the President's Desk. Plenty of worries and difficult problems. But such has been my portion for a long time — The result is that this (today) like a continuation of one I've been doing since July '41 — even before that!

Thursday, January 22

After asking the new president whether it would be OK, rodeo and movie cowboy Montie Montana tossed a lasso around him as delighted Inauguration parade spectators and not-so-delighted Secret Service personnel looked on.

"I shall go to Korea."

Dwight Eisenhower, Republican presidential nominee, made that announcement in a campaign stop in Detroit on October 24, 1952. That was the day, many now believe, that the presidential election essentially ended. Who better to resolve the stalemate in Korean than the general who commanded Allied forces in World War II?

Biographer Michael Korda calls the trip as much a warning signal for China and North Korea as it was an election strategy. The threat of a "widened war without restraints on the type of weapons used," Korda argues, had considerable effect coming from a celebrated general.

On November 29, less than a month after the election, the president-elect flew to Korea. The trip lasted three days, during which he flew over the front and visited troops. The visit, wrote historian Stephen Ambrose, showed Eisenhower the considerable might of the Chinese military and helped convince him that a renewed offensive would not work. After he took office two months later, U.S. Air Force squadrons in the region were upgraded, and nuclear warheads were sent to Okinawa. Ultimately, the Chinese and North Koreans resumed negotiations. Ambrose called the subsequent armistice of July 1953 one of Eisenhower's greatest achievements.

The president-elect reviewed Korean troops in late 1952.

THE COLD WAR: UNENDING STORY OF THE 50S

Constant jostling between the postwar superpowers, the United States and the Soviet Union, dominated the 1950s and the Eisenhower Administration. Although the competition began before Eisenhower's presidency and continued long after, the Cold War formed the context of the decade.

Eisenhower's two terms began with his visit to Korea in 1952 and stretched through the collapse of the Paris superpower summit in 1960 after the Soviets shot down an American spy plane.

Amid those came:

* Fear of betrayal, fed by the trials and executions of Julius and Ethel Rosenberg for passing U.S. atomic secrets to the Soviets.

* Sen. Joseph McCarthy's much-publicized hunt for Communists in the U.S. government.

* Astounding growth of the nuclear arsenals of the United States and the Soviet Union.

* Nationwide anxiety about the threat of nuclear war, spurring the establishment and stocking of bomb shelters in schools and other public buildings – and leading some families to build their own underground shelters.

THE ROSENBERGS...

In 1951 Julius and Ethel Rosenberg were convicted of giving atomic secrets to the Soviet Union and were sentenced to death. In February 1953, a month after he became president, Eisenhower denied the Rosenbergs' plea for clemency. Their crime, he said, involved "the deliberate betrayal of an entire nation."

The Rosenbergs' conviction was based heavily on the testimony of Ethel's brother and sister-in-law, and many doubted that the government's evidence was strong enough. Not until decades later, in the 1990s, did the U.S. government release cables that it had intercepted during World War II from the Soviet embassy in New York to the KGB. The cables – which pointed directly to Julius Rosenberg's involvement – were withheld from the trial to keep the Soviets from learning about the United States' code-breaking capabilities.

Among the many who petitioned Eisenhower to spare the Rosenbergs was Ethel Rosenberg herself.

Facing page: Not long before her execution, Ethel Rosenberg sent this handwritten plea to the president.

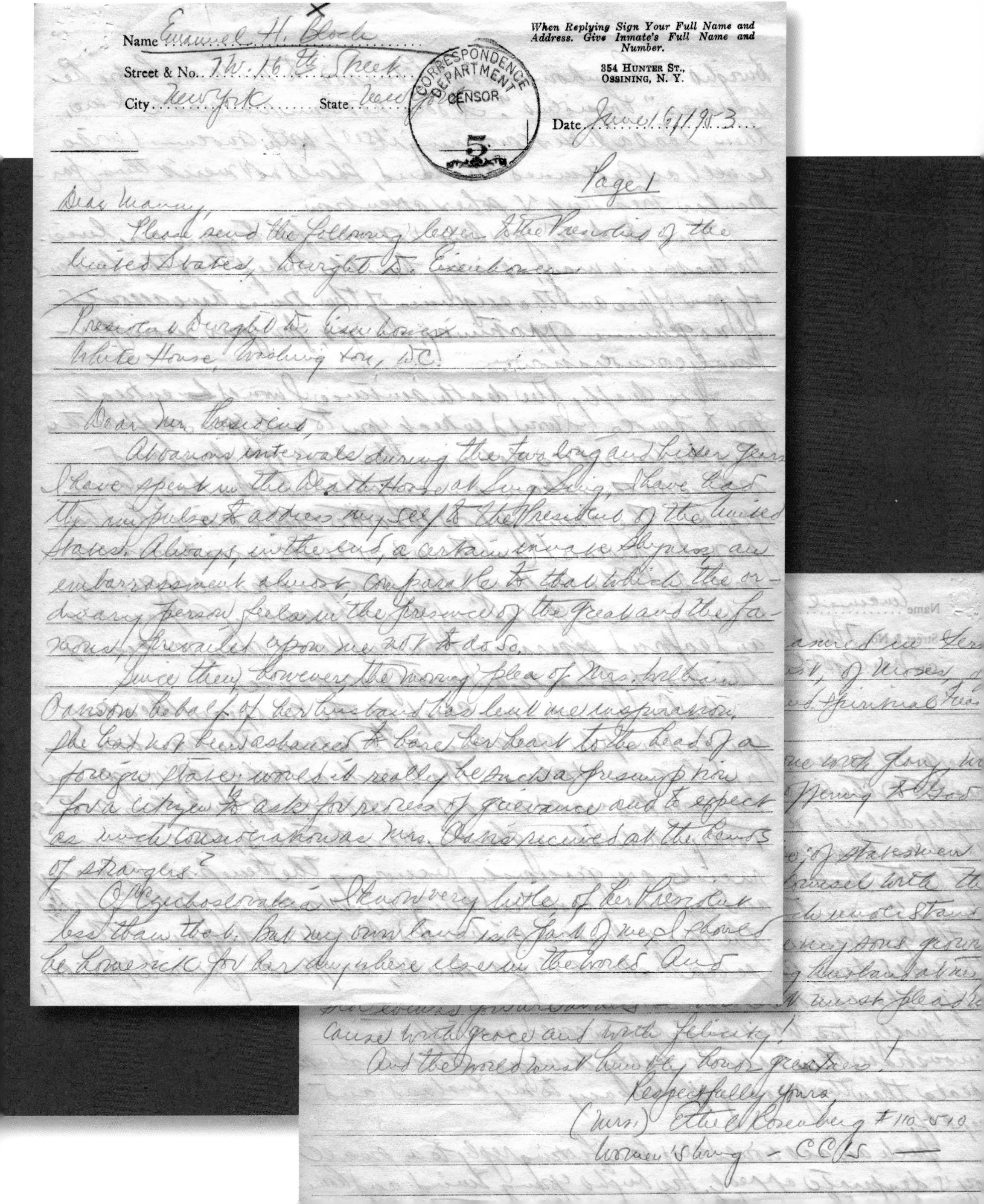

When Replying Sign Your Full Name and Address. Give Inmate's Full Name and Number.

354 Hunter St., Ossining, N. Y.

Name Emanuel H. Bloch

Street & No. 7 W. 16th Street

City New York State New York

CORRESPONDENCE DEPARTMENT CENSOR 5

Date June 16, 1953

Page 1

Dear Manny,

Please send the following letter to the President of the United States, Dwight D. Eisenhower.

President Dwight D. Eisenhower
White House, Washington, D.C.

Dear Mr. President,

At various intervals during the two long and bitter years I have spent in the Death House at Sing Sing, I have had the impulse to address myself to the President of the United States. Always, in the end, a certain innate shyness, an embarrassment almost, comparable to that which the ordinary person feels in the presence of the great and the famous, prevailed upon me not to do so.

Since then, however, the moving plea of Mrs. William Oatis on behalf of her husband has lent me inspiration. She had not been ashamed to bare her heart to the head of a foreign state; would it really be such a presumption for a citizen to ask for redress of grievance and to expect as much consideration as Mrs. Oatis received at the hands of strangers?

Of Czechoslovakia I know very little, of her President less than that, but my own land is a part of me; I should be homesick for her anywhere else in the world. And

…

cause with grace and with felicity!

And the world must humbly honor greatness!

Respectfully yours,

(Mrs.) Ethel Rosenberg #110-510

Women's Wing – C.C. 5

> "In no single instance has there been any suggestion...that there was any factor in the case which justified intervention on the part of the Executive...."

... AND THEIR BACKERS

Others also asked Eisenhower to intervene on behalf of the Rosenbergs. Among them was Clyde Miller, a professor at Columbia University, who asked Eisenhower to consider saving the two to enhance America's reputation around the world.

Eisenhower declined. Nothing, he wrote Miller, indicated "that the evidence was insufficient."

The Rosenbergs were electrocuted on June 19, 1953.

Facing page: A carbon copy of the letter sent from Eisenhower to Clyde Miller

June 10, 1953.

Personal and Confidential

Dear Clyde:

Thank you very much for your thoughts on the Rosenberg conviction. It is extremely difficult to reach a sound decision in such instances. Not all the arguments are on either side.

I started studying the record of the case immediately after Inauguration, and have had innumerable conferences on it with my associates.

Several of the obvious facts which must not be forgotten are these. The record has been reviewed and re-reviewed by every appropriate court in the land, extending over a period of more than two years. In no single instance has there been any suggestion that it was improperly tried, that the rights of the accused were violated, that the evidence was insufficient, or that there was any factor in the case which justified intervention on the part of the Executive with the function of juridical agencies.

As to any intervention based on considerations of America's reputation or standing in the world, you have given the case for one side. What you did not suggest was the need for considering this kind of argument over and against the known convictions of Communist leaders that free governments -- and especially the American government -- are notoriously weak and fearful and that consequently subversive and other kind of activity can be conducted against them with no real fear of dire punishment on the part of the perpetrator. It is, of course, important to the Communists to have this contention sustained and justified. In the present case they have even

Personal and Confidential

THE McCARTHY PROBLEM

Even before he entered the White House, Eisenhower was embroiled in the furor surrounding Sen. Joseph McCarthy.

For nearly two years McCarthy had commanded national attention by charging that the federal government was being undermined by Communists and their sympathizers. He even suggested that George C. Marshall – Army chief of staff in World War II and secretary of state under President Harry Truman – had been a dupe of the Communists.

In October 1952 Eisenhower traveled to Wisconsin, McCarthy's home state, to make a campaign speech in Milwaukee. Eisenhower planned to reassure listeners that he would have no part in indicting individuals "except under methods that were accepted as in harmony with American ideals and practices." The text speech included a paragraph supporting Marshall.

However, local Republicans as well as members of Eisenhower's staff worried that defending Marshall in Wisconsin might alienate McCarthy supporters and possibly throw the state to the Democrats in the presidential election.

The paragraph was deleted, scratched out in two separate drafts.

According to his 1963 memoir, *Mandate for Change*, Eisenhower agreed to the change. He acknowledged that critics complained he had capitulated to McCarthy supporters, but that "this was, of course, completely untrue."

Truman admired Marshall and believed that in Milwaukee that night Eisenhower had betrayed his wartime boss.

"The incident shocked even some of the General's supporters," wrote presidential biographer Michael Beschloss, "who wondered whether he was so cowed by McCarthy that he would not use his unassailable prestige to cut the demagogue down to size."

For the record, Wisconsin went Republican in 1952, with almost 61 percent voting for the GOP ticket headed by Eisenhower.

Shaking hands with Joseph McCarthy on a fateful campaign visit to Milwaukee in October 1952. Right: The paragraph famously omitted.

Sixth Draft - Communism and Freedom

To defend freedom, in short, is -- first of all -- to respect freedom. That respect demands another, quite simple kind of respect -- respect for the integrity of fellow citizens who enjoy their right to disagree. The right to question a man's judgment carries with it no automatic right to question his honor.

With respect to one case I shall be quite specific. I know that Charges of disloyalty have in the past been levelled against General George C. Marshall. Any of his alleged errors in judgment while serving in capacities other than military, I am not here discussing. But I was privileged throughout the years of World War II to know General Marshall personally, as Chief of Staff of the Army. I know him, as a man and a soldier, to be dedicated with singular selflessness and the profoundest patriotism to the service of America. Here we have a sobering lesson of the way freedom must not defend itself.

Armed with this clear and uncompromising respect for freedom, how then shall we defend it?

November 28, 1953 (Saturday)

1. Talked with Hagerty about whole McCarthy business, and voiced my grave unhappiness. Hagerty said that the whole matter would be brought up at Monday staff meeting, so decided to save until then my statement regarding the Reston quote and the general subject.

2. Redrafted first section of Wheaties II. Gave copy to AWD that afternoon.

November 29, 1953 (Sunday)

Gave my copy of Wheaties to Foster Dulles.

Also had talk with Foster, who was profoundly perturbed about McCarthy business, because it messes up his affairs. He is worried about Presidential leadership. He intended to talk to the President first thing Monday morning about what the line should be on McCarthy because of the attack on the State Dept. He also told me two terrifying facts -- (1) as of Thanksgiving Day the President had not read the McCarthy speech or been briefed on it. Dulles quote -- "The President asked me if I thought he should read it". Fact #2 -- as of Sunday afternoon, Herbert Brownell had not read the McCarthy speech. This place is really falling apart.

"President read my text with great irritation, slammed it back at me and said he would not refer to McCarthy personally – 'I will not get in the gutter with that guy.'"

C.D. Jackson, a special assistant to the president early in the Eisenhower administration, kept a log of events that in autumn 1953 centered on what to do about Sen. Joseph McCarthy. In it, the president was depicted as slowly shifting from a desire to stay out of the fray to attempting to do something about the senator. Hagerty was Press Secretary James Hagerty. Foster Dulles was Secretary of State John Foster Dulles.

December 2, 1953 (Wednesday)

1. Got to office 7:45 in order rework Pesident's statement. 8 o'clocktelephone --
    no staff meeting. Conclusion: "They are trying to freeze me out". Rushed
    over and found them all assembled unofficially in Snyder's office,
    and we went at it again.

    Morgan had moved up considerably. Shanley tried to see Pesident alone
    with Snyder, but we all trooped in with Tom Stephens' assistance, and the
    fight was on.

    Prexy read their current draft with visible irritation, and made some
    mumbling comments. Jack Martin then pitched in with great courage and
    said that a vacuum existed in this country, and it was a political vacuum,
    and unless the President filled it somebody else would fill it. The President
    twisted and squirmed, but Martin stuck to his point. I pitched in as
    strongly as I could by telling him that so long as Taft was alive he might
    have been able to get out of the responsibility of leading the Party, but
    now he could no longer get out of it, and that the people were waiting
    for a sign, and a simple sign -- and now was the time.

    Big hassle over text started. President read my text with great irritation,
    slammed it back at me and said he would not refer to McCarthy personally --
    "I will not get in the gutter with that guy".

    But gradually an interesting thing developed. The needling and the goosing
    began to take effect, and the President himself began very ably to firm
    up the text as he re-read it again, this time very carefully.

    Everyone's mood began to change from divided snarling into united help-
    ing him along, and when Prexy dictated the last paragraph exactly as it
    finally appeared, which contained the real Republican leadership gimmick,
    the group almost cheered.

    So what started as a ghastly mess turned out fine. Problem now is, having
    zippered the toga of Republican political leadership on the President's
    shoulders, how to keep that zipper shut.

2. OCB lunch

3. Mallory Brown on OCB matters.

4. Robert Taylor (Collier's) on the President's day.

5. Bill Hale -- to say hello.

CAPTURED AMERICANS

The delicate matter of Americans imprisoned by Communist countries dogged Dwight Eisenhower from his first day as president.

That day, Jan. 21, 1953, came news that Communist Chinese fighter planes had shot down a United States reconnaissance aircraft over Manchuria.

"We knew it had been missing," Eisenhower wrote years later. "Now we knew that 14 crew members had parachuted out: three had been killed and 11 taken prisoner."

Other patrol flights were lost in 1955, 1956 and 1958. In summer 1960, near the end of Eisenhower's second term, the Soviets revealed that an apparently lost American patrol plane had been shot down with two crew members captured and three missing. Often the fates of American service members remained unknown.

In 1953, after the armistice of the Korean War, American officials estimated that 944 soldiers and other military personnel were unaccounted for.

In August, 1955, while signing an order prescribing a code of conduct for armed forces members while in combat or captivity, the president said, "No American prisoner of war will be forgotten by the United States."

There's plenty of evidence that Eisenhower did not forget them. In memos kept at the Eisenhower Library, Dulles detailed the best estimates of American civilian and military personnel then being held in China and the Soviet Union.

Even today, the fate of many remains mysterious. In 1996, North Korea allowed a United States team to search for remains of American soldiers. By 2005, more than 220 sets of remains had been uncovered.

Facing page: A chilling memo quoted a Soviet defector's claim that certain American and other U.N. POW's would be trained to work in the United States as agents of the Communists.

Office Memorandum • UNITED STATES GOVERNMENT

TO : EO - Mr. Staats

FROM : SPS - Dr. Craig

DATE: 31 January 1955

SUBJECT: Interview with Rastvorov (former MVD) concerning U.S. Prisoners of War in the USSR

 On Friday, 28 January 1955, a meeting was arranged between members of the Special Projects Staff and Mr. Rastvorov. General Dale O. Smith was also present. The interview was on the subject of U.S. prisoners of war being held by the Soviets.

 Mr. Rastvorov made the following important points bearing upon the subject:

 1. He was told by recent arrivals (1950-1953) from the Soviet Union to the USSR's Tokyo mission that U.S. and other UN POW's were being held in Siberia.

 2. The POW's will be screened by the Soviets and trained to be illegal residents in U.S. or other countries where they can live as Americans.

 3. Selected POW's will be used in propaganda work.

 4. Use will be made of the identities and biographies of dead POW's in preparing legends for new Soviet agents.

 5. The mechanism for POW control in Korea was headed by the Soviets.

 6. The sentencing of the eleven U.S. POW's charged with espionage by the Chinese Communists was conceived and directed by the Soviets. The release of other Americans in Europe was part of this plot.

OCB:SPSPJCorso:mas

SECRET

July 18, 1955

MEMORANDUM FOR THE PRESIDENT

Subject: Americans Detained in the Soviet Union

The American people share with other peoples of the world
a real concern about the imprisonment of some of their countrymen in the Soviet Union. Most of these persons have been held
since World War II. It is time to liquidate problems rising
out of that War so that we may proceed with greater mutual
trust to the solution of major issues facing the world today.

Of greatest concern to American people are reports reaching the United States about Americans still being held in
Soviet prison camps. The American Embassy in Moscow has made
many representations on this subject. While we appreciate the
recent release of several Americans, others still remain in
Soviet custody. On July 16 the American Embassy in Moscow
gave the Foreign Office a list of eight American citizens
about whose detention in the Soviet Union we have information
from returning prisoners of war. Any action you would take
to bring about the early release of these particular persons
would help relations between our countries.

We have also received a number of reports from returning
European prisoners of war that members of the crew of the
U.S. Navy Privateer, shot down over the Baltic Sea on April 18,
1950, are alive and in Soviet prison camps. We are asking for
their repatriation and that of other American citizens being
held in the Soviet Union not only because of general humani-
tarian principles, but also because such action is called for
under the Litvinov-Roosevelt Agreement of 1933.

John Foster Dulles

Secretary of State Dulles
sent these accounts of
Communist prisoners to the
president. Many had been
held since World War II.

Destroy

July 18, 1955

MEMORANDUM FOR THE PRESIDENT

...War II Prisoners Detained in the Soviet U...

...n of World War II prisoners of war still b...
...iet Union is one of great concern not only...
...nd countrymen of these prisoners but to th...
...he release of the thousands of German, Ital...
...risoners of war and smaller numbers of Aust...
..., Dutch, Norwegian and Spanish prisoners w...
...se of anguish and would help to establish...
...utual confidence which we both agree is...
...he solution of major problems facing us no...
...iet Government will take early steps in th...

For information only: Estimated Numbers of prisoners of
detained in the USSR.

West Germans	138,000
Italians	50,000
Japanese	1,452 known alive
	12,642 missing
Austrians	447
Belgians	5
Danes	...
Dutch	816
Norwegians	5 (about)
Spanish	68

1. Americans detained in the Soviet Union are neither being
held as prisoners of war nor as "war criminals".

2. The Soviet Government has claimed that it is no longer
holding World War II prisoners but it has admitted that it
is still detaining some "war criminals".

July 18, 1955

MEMORANDUM FOR THE PRESIDENT

ject: Americans Imprisoned or Detained in Communist China

In raising this subject with the Russians, it is
ommended that you express our great continuing concern over
failure of the Chinese Communists to release these Americans.
would hope that the Soviet leaders would exercise their
luence with Peiping to get these Americans out promptly.

There are some 38 civilians and 11 military personnel
ll detained. We were encouraged by the release of the four
ers on May 31. Yet, that was only a first step. The
ted States Government and people feel strongly that these
. citizens should be promptly released. There should be
oubt about the nation-wide feeling on this issue. The
nese Communists may intend to try to extract concessions
the release of any or all of these Americans. The United
tes rejects such use of human beings for political purposes.

We continue to hope that the efforts during many months
the United Nations Secretary General, the British, and
r governments, as well as our own direct efforts, will
g results quickly. We would welcome Soviet efforts to
ect this serious injustice.

If the Russians mention the Chinese Commun
United States is holding Chinese students a
, and mistreating them, they should be told
Chinese students who wish to leave the Unit
given permission to do so. They have been
to move around the country, and helped fin
he United States.

John Foster D

This table showed where American service personnel were being held.

IAC-D-101
24 January 1956

Y

THE JOINT CHIEFS OF STAFF
Washington 25, D. C.

DDIM-6-56
11 January 1956

MORANDUM FOR: Chairman, Intelligence Advisory Committee

ect   : Intelligence Requirements on U.S. Citizens
                Held in Sino-Soviet Bloc Countries

1.   In a memorandum, dated 21 November 1955, addressed
e Deputy Director for Intelligence, the Joint Staff, the
stant to the Secretary of Defense (Special Operations) requested
Joint Intelligence Committee to "make a study of the intelligence
irements for an effective prisoner identification and repatriation
ram and make recommendations for its adoption."

2.   The results of this study indicate certain intelligence
ction and production requirements which should be satisfied.
study addressed itself primarily to the consideration of un-
unted for prisoners of war and other missing people who are
duals after all normal accounting processes, prisoner ex-

IAC-D-101
24 January 1956

ANNEX

STATISTICAL BREAKDOWN OF MISSING PERSONS

	Communist China	USSR & Eur. Sats.	Total
Civilians	14	1	15
Army	244	10	254
Navy	3	10	13
Air Force	190	33	223
Marine Corps	13	-	13
Coast Guard	-	-	-
	464	54	518

HEART ATTACK

In the predawn hours of Sept. 24, 1955, while vacationing in Colorado, Dwight Eisenhower awoke with severe chest pains. Treated by his physician, he went back to sleep. By the middle of the day, an electrocardiogram found that he had suffered a heart attack, and the president was taken to a Denver hospital.

Before the end of the year he was back at work in the White House, with this caution from doctors: Avoid irritation, frustration, anxiety, fear and, above all, anger.

In a letter to Abilene friend "Swede" Hazlett, Eisenhower dismissed that advice:

"Just what do you think the Presidency is?'"

Levity aside, Eisenhower was troubled by his heart attack. During recovery at Fitzsimmons Army Hospital in Denver, it was his duty to put on a brave face for the sake of the nation. He faced photographers from his wheelchair, wearing a shirt with the message "Much Better, Thanks" over his heart.

Yet the president had undergone immense pain.

"I never told Mamie how much it hurt," he confided to his vice president, Richard Nixon.

Eisenhower accepted the best wishes of acquaintances such as comedians Bud Abbott and Lou Costello. He also accepted the wisdom of four doctors who visited him in his Denver hospital room to advise him to avoid tobacco. All of them, according to Eisenhower biographer Stephen Ambrose, were smoking at the time.

After seven weeks of rest, he returned to the White House in November.

The litany of Eisenhower's ailments over the years make his service to the country seem only more heroic.

In the early 1930s, serving under Gen. Douglas MacArthur,

Facing page, top: Eisenhower on the sun deck of a Denver hospital.

Below: The comedy team of Abbott and Costello, with a reference to their famous "Who's on First?" baseball routine, sent best wishes. They received a reply, right, probably signed by Mamie Eisenhower.

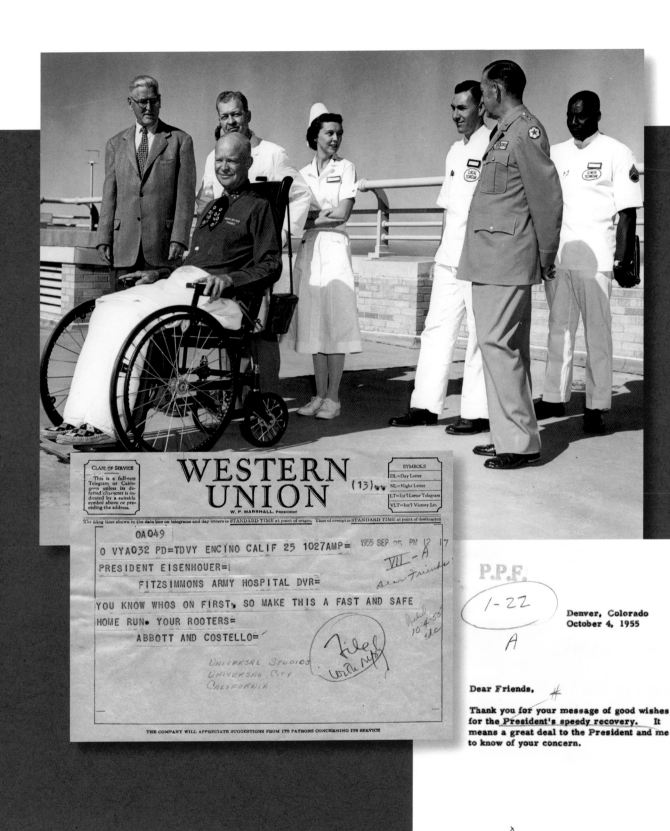

WESTERN UNION

(13)

W. P. MARSHALL, PRESIDENT

CLASS OF SERVICE

This is a full-rate Telegram or Cablegram unless its deferred character is indicated by a suitable symbol above or preceding the address.

SYMBOLS

DL=Day Letter
NL=Night Letter
LT=Int'l Letter Telegram
VLT=Int'l Victory Ltr.

The filing time shown in the date line on telegrams and day letters is STANDARD TIME at point of origin. Time of receipt is STANDARD TIME at point of destination.

OA049

O VYA032 PD=TDVY ENCINO CALIF 25 1027AMP=   1955 SEP 25 PM 12 17

PRESIDENT EISENHOUER=

FITZSIMMONS ARMY HOSPITAL DVR=

YOU KNOW WHOS ON FIRST, SO MAKE THIS A FAST AND SAFE

HOME RUN. YOUR ROOTERS=

ABBOTT AND COSTELLO=

UNIVERSAL STUDIOS
UNIVERSAL CITY
CALIFORNIA

THE COMPANY WILL APPRECIATE SUGGESTIONS FROM ITS PATRONS CONCERNING ITS SERVICE

P.P.F.

1-22

A

Denver, Colorado
October 4, 1955

Dear Friends,

Thank you for your message of good wishes
for the President's speedy recovery.   It
means a great deal to the President and me
to know of your concern.

Mr. Bud Abbott
Mr. Lou Costello
Universal Studios
Universal City
California

he suffered indigestion, back pain, bursitis and hemorrhoids. During World War II, with the weight of the Allied war effort in Europe upon him, he had smoked four packs of cigarettes a day and enjoyed virtually no exercise or relaxation.

Early in 1956, less than half a year after the heart attack, Eisenhower decided to run for re-election. That June, he was diagnosed with ileitis, a chronic inflammation of the intestines. An operation bypassed the diseased section of his small intestine. In November he was swept back into office. One year later he suffered a stroke that briefly left him slightly paralyzed and with impaired speech. By then, one biographer has written, Eisenhower was receiving 10 minutes of oxygen a day.

Presidential physician Howard Snyder recorded in his private journal in December 1958 how Eisenhower asked him to check his blood pressure. During the routine procedure, Snyder wrote, "he cussed the doctors who had encouraged him to accept a second term."

Although he preferred not to be photographed smoking, some photos captured Eisenhower with a cigarette in the 1940s, top and facing page, and in the 1930s, right.

OFFICE OF RICHARD E. BYRD

April 1, 1955

Dear Mr. President:

     For appointing me officer in charge of the upcoming expedition you have my deep and everlasting gratitude. I will serve you to the best of my ability.

     There are now many nations interested in Antarctica - five of them demonstrate a passionate interest.

     It is, therefore, another area where there may be international trouble for you.

     Over the years I have attemp[...] friction down to a minimum and have m[...] with other countries. I shall not only c[...] efforts in that direction but by friendly [...] and cooperation in scientific fields, we [...] help by creating international goodwill.

     Antarctica exploration is pop[...] people of this nation are grateful to you[...] ful of this nation's interest in that area[...]

     With warm regard.

        Respectfull[...]

        Richard E. [...]

The President
The White House
Washington, D. C.

RICHARD EVELYN BYRD

April 1, 1955

Dear Mr. President:

I have for some time wanted you to have something that I have taken with me on all of my journeys of exploration and scientific endeavors in far places.

I am enclosing a St. Anthony and a St. Christopher that were given to me by a Catholic Priest. (I am an Episcopalian.)

I had these items with me on all of my six expeditions to the polar regions which began near the North Pole in 1925.

They were with me on the first flight to the North Pole and also on the first one to the South Pole.

They were with me on the transatlantic flight when Colonel Lindbergh beat me to France.

They were with me for the long winter night of 1934 during my lonely vigil for science that I spent in the shadow of the South Pole.

They were with me also on the flights on which I discovered more than a million square miles of hitherto unknown area (this figure includes the unknown ice-covered sea area). Henceforth I shall take with me the knife you gave me. It is certainly a useful item.

With warm regard.

        Sincerely,

        Richard E. Byrd

P.S.   I have been for some time writing a thesis to show as exactly as I can what the fundamental basic mistake is that we as a people have made within. If I can succeed in showing this it will, I believe, demonstrate more clearly why, for several years to come, more bipartisan action is called for.

The President
The White House
Washington, D. C.

In the 1950s, long-time polar adventurer Richard Byrd was named officer-in-charge of Operation Deep Freeze, an exploration of Antarctica. The appointment led to this correspondence between him and President Eisenhower. The medals to which Byrd and Eisenhower referred are in the collection of the Eisenhower Library and Museum.

April 5, 1955

Dear Dick:

I cannot tell you how touched I am by your two letters of April first. I am highly complimented that you should want me to have the St. Anthony and the St. Christopher medals that have carried you safely through so many perilous journeys, and I am, of course, delighted to accept them.

At the same time, might I be bold enough to suggest that I "lend" them back to you for your forthcoming trip? My prayers will go with you for your safety and success, and I would be a little bit happier to know that you have with you once again your familiar and valued little medals. If you are willing, I should like to return them to you until after your return.

I hope you will share with me your thesis to demonstrate the "fundamental basic mistake" we have made. You know how strongly I, for one, urge bipartisan, or non-partisan, action.

With warm regard,

Sincerely,

Rear Admiral Richard E. Byrd
The Hay-Adams House
Washington, D. C.

4/15/55
Adm. Byrd phoned from Boston. Said he'd have a representative pick up the medals. Cdr. Dustin (from Pentagon) got them from Guard, Northwest Gate, about 3:15 this afternoon.

hew

CIVIL RIGHTS

Dwight Eisenhower's freshman class at Abilene High School was integrated.

As a youth, Eisenhower once wrote, members of his football team threatened not to line up against an opposing team that included an African-American player. Eisenhower, according to a story he recorded years later, volunteered to line up across from the black player, and later shook his hand.

"Rest of the team was a bit ashamed," he wrote in a journal.

Five decades later, in 1957, President Eisenhower sent U.S. Army troops to Little Rock, Arkansas, to help nine African-American students enter Central High School. Despite that dramatic act, Eisenhower's efforts on behalf of civil rights appeared to some as half-hearted.

Indeed, Eisenhower occasionally appeared to lack enthusiasm.

The record of the briefing he got before a press conference in November 1956 recorded his response to news that the Supreme Court had upheld desegregation of the public buses in Montgomery, Alabama: He was, it said, "more of a 'States Righter' than the Supreme Court."

The next year he wrote his lifelong friend "Swede" Hazlett, "I think that no other single event has so disturbed the domestic scene in many years as did the Supreme Court's decision of 1954 in the school segregation case." Some authors suggest that Eisenhower's perceived lack of activism emboldened those trying to delay desegregation of public schools.

But recently Eisenhower's civil rights legacy has been re-assessed.

In 2007, David Nichols published *A Matter of Justice: Eisenhower and the Beginning of the Civil Rights Revolution*. He emphasized not Eisenhower's rhetoric but his actions, especially in areas the president considered within his jurisdiction. Eisenhower, Nichols pointed out:

The photograph of Eisenhower's freshman class at Abilene High School shows at least two people of color. Eisenhower is at lower right.

* Encouraged the desegregation of the District of Columbia.

* Continued integration of the U.S. armed forces, initiated by Harry Truman by executive order in 1948.

* Submitted to Congress the first Civil Rights bill proposed since Reconstruction.

He signed that bill, named the Civil Rights Act of 1957. It established a federal Civil Rights Commission as well as a civil rights division in the Justice Department. Some criticized the legislation because it included provisions that made it difficult for the Justice Department to convict registrars who refused to enroll African-Americans. The Civil Rights Act of 1960, however, authorized federal judges to appoint referees to help African-Americans register to vote.

Yet Eisenhower's greatest civil rights legacy, according to Nichols, was represented in the judges he appointed to federal courts, particularly to the U.S. Supreme Court. It was that court, led by Eisenhower appointee Earl Warren, that issued the *Brown v. Board of Education* ruling striking down school segregation.

PRE-PRESS CONFERENCE BRIEFING, November 14, 1956.

Nehru visit. President hopes it will be soon -- time and place under consideration but not yet set.

Meeting with French and British.   Under discussion but no plans at the moment.

Dulles
State

Bedell

Politic
electi
say th
explar

Len H
wheth

Secon
that ir
than t
to Am
no mo
he tho

- 2 -

like ours can protect itself. It is not a simple matter like freedom of the press.   No one has the right to endanger his country. President, however, will say he has not had time to study it.

Supreme Court upheld degegregation on intra-state buses. President was reminded of decision of yesterday. This was case involving Montgomery, Alabama, private bus company operating on a public francise. President said that in some of these things he was more of a "States Righter" than the Supreme Court.   He fears that by some steps the country is going to get into trouble, and the problems of the Negroes set back, not advanced. He referred to the schools -- said how could the Federal Government inforce a ruling applying to schools supported by state funds.   Said could have a general strike in the South. Feels that even the so-called great liberals are going to have to take a second look at the whole thing.   He may say that the Supreme Court does not refer its decisions to him for approval or study. Governor of Mississippi said that they were going to ignore the ruling. President said that eventually a District Court is going to site someone for contempt, and then we are going to be up against it.

"DEAR MR. PRESIDENT..."

In 1955 a young African-American woman from Baltimore wrote President Eisenhower. For a long time, something had been puzzling her.

"Why do you and your co-workers go from your own country to another, and try to teach those people how to live with each other….When right here in America people do not have the same equal rights," she asked. "They should because the Constitution says so."

Sophie Tinsley's letter contrasting the rhetoric of American democracy with the reality of the time is displayed today at the Eisenhower Library and Museum.

Sophie Tinsley enclosed a picture with her letter to the president.

acked
9/14/55
AB

118 N. Central ave.
Baltimore, 2, Md.
aug, , 1955

Dear Mr. President,

I am a 17 Year old Colored school girl. This is something that has been puzzling me for a long time. Why do You and Your Co-workers go from Your own Country to another, and try to teach those people how to live with each other, and with out war and try to get them to turn Certain prisoner free. When right here in america people donot have the Same equal rights. They should because the Constitution says so. To a Certain extent they do but the negroes do not have the same liberty as the white peoples. The whites in the south are still Killing negroes and getting a little time in Jail if any at all. But let A Colored person Kill a white one and they get Killed themself if the law don't Kill them the white people will. Places are still Jim Crowed a Colored person can't set beside a white one on the train from washington to Virginia but one of those same Colored people can go in their Kitchen and Cook food for them and they set down and eat it. If we are so what every we are suppose to me its a wonder we in someway would not harm their food (smile) Right here in Maryland there is still a difference made between us. The white people have to advantage over us. Why? We are men and women — human beings the same as the Suppose those people of other nations say how can you talk about how other people should live together and freedom. as well as no more wars. When right here in The United States there are people who are not fully free. Meaning the Negroes What about the Negro? I wish I could truly see the difference people find in us except for our color. The are good people as well as bad ones in every race. I hope there is no harm in my writing this letter I was thinking who can I talk about this to to recive a good answer and just started to write. I enjoy studing the people of my race history or Jim Crow right up to today and believe me the books do no leave a pretty picture. Here is a small picture of myself just in case you wonder what I look like. —————— Thank, You,

Sophie Tinsley

LAKEVILLE FARM
BOYCE, VA.
FEB. 12, 1956

DEAR MR. EISENHOWER,

I AM NINE YEARS OLD AND I AM WHITE BUT I HAVE MANY FEELINGS ABOUT SEGREGATION. WHY SHOULD PEOPLE FEEL THAT WAY BECAUSE THE COLOR OF THE SKIN? IF I PAINTED MY FACE BLACK I WOULDN'T BE LET IN ANY PUBLIC SCHOOLS etc. MY FEELINGS HAVEN'T CHANGED, JUST THE COLOR OF MY SKIN.

LONG AGO ON CHRISTMAS DAY JESUS CHRIST WAS BORN. AS YOU REMEMBER HE WAS BORN TO SAVE THE WORLD. NOT ONLY WHITE PEOPLE BUT BLACK YELLOW RED AND BROWN.

COLORED PEOPLE AREN'T GIVEN A CHANCE. "THEY DON'T HAVE A GOOD EDUCATION," SAYS MANY PEOPLE. IS IT THEIR FAULT IF THEIR FATHERS ARE SO POOR THEY MUST BE TAKEN OUT AT AN EARLY AGE TO FIND JOBS? ONLY ABOUT 20% of OUR PREP SCHOOLS ARE FOR COLORED PEOPLE. SO WHAT IF THEIR SKIN IS BLACK? THEY STILL HAVE FEELINGS BUT MOST OF ALL

PLEASE MR. EISENHOWER, PLEASE TRY AND HAVE SCHOOLS AND OTHER THINGS ACCEPT COLORED PEOPLE.

SINCERLY,

CATHERINE DREW GILPIN

Another young person who wrote the president was a 9-year-old white resident of Virginia, Drew Gilpin. She also described herself as confused:

"If I painted my face black I wouldn't be let in any public schools, etc. My feelings haven't changed, just the color of my skin."

In a remarkable postscript half a century later, the author of that letter asked the Eisenhower Library staff to see whether they could find it. They did, and in a 2003 essay Drew Gilpin Faust – then professor of history and dean of the Radcliffe Institute for Advanced Study – discussed the opportunity she got by living in "specific historical moments."

In her case, the moment was the civil rights struggle of the 1950s.

"Had I been born a decade earlier," she wrote, "I would never have asked those questions, written that letter, or been privileged to lead what has become my life."

In 2007 Drew Gilpin Faust was named president of Harvard University, the first woman to hold that job.

HELP FROM THE PULPIT

In the middle 1950s, President Eisenhower sought guidance on civil rights from a Baptist preacher in the American South whose name was familiar to millions — Billy Graham. In years to come, Graham would become known as a preacher to the presidents.

Eisenhower's request to Graham in March 1956 was specific. He asked Graham to promote racial tolerance and progress in race relations from the pulpit, and wondered whether other ministers could follow his lead.

"Ministers know that peacemakers are blessed," Eisenhower wrote Graham, "they should also know that the most effective peacemaker is one who prevents a quarrel from developing."

Graham responded with enthusiasm, saying he was convening an Atlanta conference among leaders of several major southern denominations and that he would share Eisenhower's suggestions with them.

What some commentators later criticized Eisenhower for – not being outspoken on behalf of civil rights – Graham found wise.

"Your deeds are speaking for you," he told Eisenhower. "You have so wonderfully kept above the controversies that necessarily raged from time to time."

Eisenhower and Graham maintained their relationship. One of the last visitors to Eisenhower's room at Walter Reed Hospital in Washington before the former president's death in 1969 was Graham.

Eisenhower's question to the famous minister: "Can an old sinner like me ever go to heaven?"

Eisenhower and Billy Graham. Facing page: Carbon copy of a letter the president sent to the evangelist.

March 22, 1956

PERSONAL

Dear Billy:

I have been urgently thinking about the matters we discussed in our conversation the day before yesterday.   I
refer particularly to that part of our talk that dealt with
the opportunity open to ministers of promoting both
tolerance and progress in our race relations problems.
I think we agreed, for example, that they could discuss
the mounting evidence of steady progress toward elimination of racial difficulties, even though all reasonable men
appreciate that eventual and complete success will not be
attained for some years.   Ministers know that peacemakers
are blessed; they should also know that the most effective
peacemaker is one who prevents a quarrel from developing,
rather than one who has to pick up the pieces remaining
after an unfortunate fight.

As I told you, my mind constantly turns to the ease with
which effective steps might be taken in the adult as compared to the juvenile field.   Of course the kind of evidence
that we should like to see pile up is the kind that would convince Federal District judges in the several localities that
progress is real.   All of us realize, I think, that success
through conciliation will be more lasting and stronger than
could be attained through force and conflict.

Certain questions occur to me that might be worth your
consideration:

a.   Could we not begin to elect a few qualified Negroes
        to school boards ?

b.   The same to City Commissioners ?

c.   The same to County Commissioners ?

d.   Could not universities begin to make entrance into
       their graduate schools strictly on the basis of
       merit -- the examinations to be conducted by some
       Board which might even be unaware of the race or
       color of the applicant?

e.   Could there be introduced flexible plans for filling
       up public conveyances so that we do not have the
       spectacle of Negroes in considerable numbers
       waiting for a ride on a public conveyance, while
       numerous seats are held vacant for possible white
       customers?

It would appear to me that things like this could properly be
mentioned in a pulpit.   Another thought that occurs to me
is that you might express some admiration for the Catholic
Archbishop, Joseph Francis Rummel, in Louisiana, who
had the courage to desegregate his parochial schools.
Such approval on your part would not necessarily imply
that the same thing could be done in all schools and without
delay.   You would merely be pointing out that in a special
case, and under the strict supervision possible in privately
supported schools, one man had the courage to give this
kind of integration a good trial to determine the results.

Likewise there could be approval expressed concerning the
progress made in certain areas in the border States, and
in all other areas in the South where any type of advance at
all has been effected.   Thus these things would be called
to the attention of Federal judges, who themselves would
be inclined to operate moderately and with complete regard
for the sensibilities of the population.

This letter does not require an answer; it is merely
some thoughts that have occurred to me on the subject.
It constitutes gratuitous advice -- and is probably worth
exactly what all that kind of advice usually is.

With warm personal regard,

                              Sincerely,

The Reverend Billy Graham
Pennsylvania Building
13th Street & Pennsylvania Avenue, N. W.
Washington, D. C.

THE WHITE HOUSE
MAR 29 3 25 PM '56
RECEIVED

*The President
The White House
Washington, D.C.*

Dear Mr. President:

It was a delight to talk with you last Tuesday in Washington. I have given a great deal of thought to our discussion, particularly as to the race question. Yesterday I received your letter outlining suggestions. Please be assured that I shall keep both your letter and our conversations in confidence.

I feel with you that the Church must take a place of spiritual leadership in this crucial matter that confronts not only the South but the entire nation. You will be interested to know that I am taking immediate steps to call the outstanding leaders of the major Southern denominations together as soon as possible in Atlanta for a conference on this subject. I shall outline to them your suggestions for racial understanding and progress. In addition, I will do all in my power to urge Southern ministers to call upon the people for moderation, charity, compassion and progress toward compliance with the Supreme Court decision. Your own personal suggestions are excellent.

The great denominational conventions will be held during May, and by that time we should have concrete suggestions to present at these assemblies and conventions that will get it before the average minister of the South, urging him to present these viewpoints from his pulpit. In this area I believe we can make a contribution toward better understanding.

Immediately after the election you can take whatever steps you feel are wise and right. In the meantime, it might be well to let the Democratic Party bear the brunt of the debate. Your deeds are speaking for you. You have so wonderfully kept above the controversies that necessarily raged from time to time. I hope particularly before November you are able to stay out of this bitter racial situation that is developing.

I had a long talk yesterday with Governor Hodges of North Carolina and Governor Frank Clement of Tennessee. I have urged them both to consider the racial problem from a spiritual point of view. They are two of our more "moderate" Southern governors.

I talked to Sid Richardson on the phone the other day. In spite of the fact that you vetoed the gas bill, he is still your biggest booster and friend.

Cordially yours,

BG:L

LITTLE ROCK BOILS OVER

In early September 1957, Dwight and Mamie Eisenhower began a vacation at the naval base in Newport, Rhode Island. The respite didn't last long. In Arkansas, Gov. Orville Faubus had called out the state's National Guard to keep black students from entering Central High School as ordered by a federal court. To try to defuse the situation, Eisenhower called Faubus to Newport for a meeting. Faubus returned to Arkansas, where he remained intransigent.

A Navy photographer captured the president and the recalcitrant Gov. Faubus at the naval base, along with a congressman from Arkansas.

number 14093
date 9-14-57
taken by: Paul Begley, PHC
location Coasters Harbor Island NEWPORT, R.I. USNaval Base vicinity of Bldg 87
subject

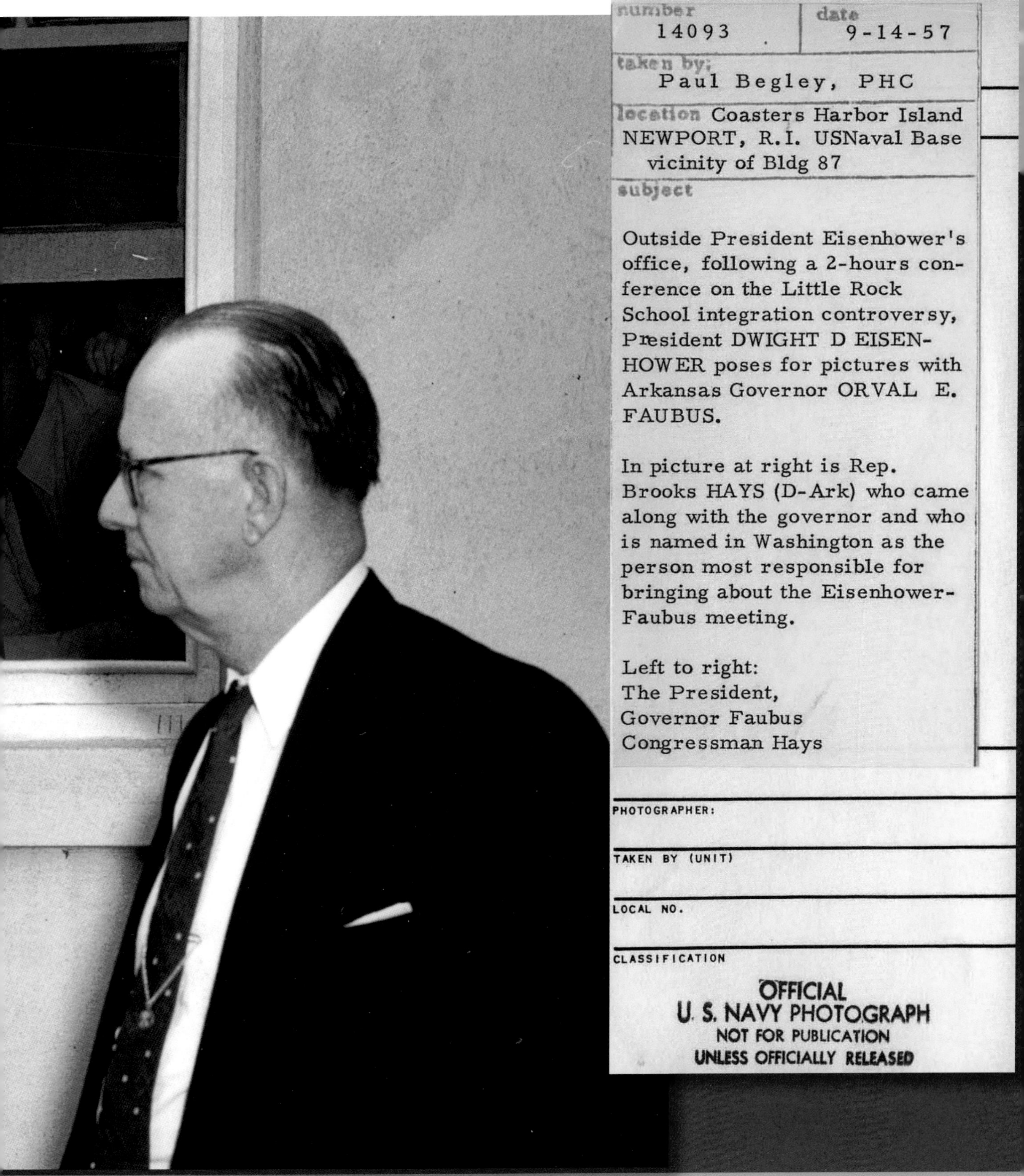

Outside President Eisenhower's office, following a 2-hours conference on the Little Rock School integration controversy, President DWIGHT D EISENHOWER poses for pictures with Arkansas Governor ORVAL E. FAUBUS.

In picture at right is Rep. Brooks HAYS (D-Ark) who came along with the governor and who is named in Washington as the person most responsible for bringing about the Eisenhower-Faubus meeting.

Left to right:
The President,
Governor Faubus
Congressman Hays

PHOTOGRAPHER:

TAKEN BY (UNIT)

LOCAL NO.

CLASSIFICATION

OFFICIAL
U. S. NAVY PHOTOGRAPH
NOT FOR PUBLICATION
UNLESS OFFICIALLY RELEASED

DDE

THE WHITE HOUSE

Troops —

not to enforce integration

but

to prevent ~~violent~~ opposition

by violence to orders of a court.

_____

In Arkansas.

Governor ordered out troops,

armed & equipped and partially

maintained by Fed. Government will

instructions ~~orders~~ to prevent execution

of a plan proposed by School Board,

approved by Fed Judge.

_____

President can stand by and

see the entire court system

disintegrate (meaning dissolution of

our form of gov't) or he can carry out

his oath of office.

On September 24, 1957, President Eisenhower ordered paratroopers of the 101st Airborne Division to Little Rock, Arkansas, from their base in Fort Campbell, Kentucky. Their task: to restore order at Central High School, where mobs had gathered to protest the desegregation of the school by nine African-American students.

Having issued that order, Eisenhower interrupted his vacation in Newport to return to Washington to address the country on radio and television. The gravity of the situation, he believed, demanded that he speak from the White House.

On the flight back, Eisenhower took a sheet of White House stationery and began organizing his thoughts. That he pondered his actions for some time is suggested by the doodles in the upper-left hand corner of the document.

Among the handwritten notes: "Troops - not to enforce integration but to prevent opposition by violence to orders of a court…"

In his speech that night, he was careful to frame his action not as federal enforcement of integration, but as upholding the federal justice system:

"Whenever normal agencies prove inadequate to the task and it becomes necessary for the executive branch of the federal government to use its powers and authority to uphold federal courts, the President's responsibility is inescapable."

Even if some Americans disagreed with the decision by the Supreme Court in *Brown v. Board of Education*, those sentiments would always be trumped by the law of the land.

"Our personal opinions about the decision," Eisenhower told the country, "have no bearing on the matter of enforcement; the responsibility and authority of the Supreme Court to interpret the Constitution are very clear."

Among many residents of Little Rock, Eisenhower's decision to intervene in the Central High School crisis in September 1957 was unpopular. But one group was deeply gratified – the parents of the nine African-American students who desegregrated the school.

In a telegram several days after federal troops arrived at Central High, W.B. Brown, speaking for the parents, told Eisenhower that he had "strengthened our faith in democracy...now as never before...."

Eisenhower responded promptly, calling his action necessary to "defend the Constitution of the United States." That, he added, was "my solemn oath as your president...."

He also offered a personal note, complimenting the parents on their courage:

"In the course of our country's progress toward equality of opportunity, you have shown dignity and courage in circumstances which would daunt citizens of lesser faith."

RECEIVED
OCT - 7 1957
The White CENTRAL FILES
Washington

WA037 NL PD

LITTLE ROCK ARK SEP 30   1957 OCT 1 AM 7 43

THE PRESIDENT

THE WHITE HOUSE

WE THE PARENTS OF NINE NEGRO CHILDREN ENROLLED AT LITTLE
ROCK CENTRAL HIGH SCHOOL WANT YOU TO KNOW THAT YOUR
ACTION IN SAFE GUARDING THEIR RIGHTS HAVE STRENGTHENED
OUR FAITH IN DEMOCRACY STOP NOW AS NEVER BEFORE WE HAVE
AN ABIDING FEELING OF BELONGING AND PURPOSEFULNESS STOP
WE BELIEVE THAT FREEDOM AND EQUALITY WITH WHICH ALL MEN

ARE ENDOWED AT BIRTH CAN BE MAINTAINED ONLY THROUGH
FREEDOM AND EQUALITY OF OPPORTUNITY FOR SELF DEVELOPMENT
GROWTH AND PURPOSEFUL CITIZENSHIP STOP WE BELIEVE THAT
THE DEGREE TO WHICH PEOPLE EVERYWHERE REALIZE AND ACCEPT
THIS CONCEPT WILL DETERMINE IN A LARGE MEASURE AMERICAS
TRUE GROWTH AND TRUE GREATNESS STOP YOU HAVE DEMONSTRATED
ADMIRABLY TO US THE NATION AND THE WORLD HOW PROFOUNDLY
YOU BELIEVE IN THIS CONCEPT STOP FOR THIS WE ARE DEEPLY
GRATEFUL AND RESPECTFULLY EXTEND TO YOU OUR HEARTFELT
AND LASTING THANKS STOP MAY THE ALMIGHTY AND ALL WISE

FATHER OF US ALL BLESS GUIDE AND KEEP YOU ALWASY
OSCAR ECKFORD JR 4405 WEST 18TH LOTHAIRE S GREEN 1224
WEST 21ST ST JUANITA WALLS 1500 VALENTINE W B BROWN
1117 RINGO LOIS M PATTILLO 1121 CROSS H C RAY 2111
CROSS ELLIS THOMAS 1214 WEST 20TH W L ROBERTS 2301
HOWARD H L MOTHERSHED 1313 CHESTER.

October 4, 1957

PERSONAL

Dear Mr. Brown:

I deeply appreciate your September thirtieth telegram,
signed also by other parents. The supreme law of our
land has been clearly defined by the Supreme Court.
To support and defend the Constitution of the United
States is my solemn oath as your President -- a pledge
which imposes upon me the responsibility to see that
the laws of our country are faithfully executed. I shall
continue to discharge that responsibility in the interest
of all Americans today, as well as to preserve our free
institutions of government for the sake of Americans
yet unborn.

I believe that America's heart goes out to you and your
children in your present ordeal. In the course of our
country's progress toward equality of opportunity, you
have shown dignity and courage in circumstances which
would daunt citizens of lesser faith.

With best wishes to you,

Sincerely,

(sgd) DWIGHT D. EISENHOWER

Mr. W. B. Brown
1117 Ringo Street
Little Rock
Arkansas

PERSONAL

(Sent to Mr. David H. Stephens, Chief Postal Inspector, Room 3426,
Post Office Dept., for delivery)

"OH NO! NOT AGAIN"

Jackie Robinson, the iconic African-American athlete who in 1947 broke Major League Baseball's color line, was a prominent African-American supporter of Republican candidates. Dwight Eisenhower, meanwhile, was not only an ardent baseball fan, having played the sport as a young man, but also a fan of the Brooklyn Dodgers, for whom Robinson played.

Nevertheless, Robinson was willing to criticize the president. In 1958, he had grown fatigued hearing Eisenhower counsel black Americans to be patient about civil rights. On the letterhead of Chock full o' Nuts, the New York coffee company for which Robinson worked after retiring from baseball, Robinson chastised the president.

"I respectfully remind you sir, that we have been the most patient of all people," he wrote. "When you said we must have self-respect, I wondered how we could have self-respect and remain patient considering the treatment accorded us through the years."

A volume of Robinson's civil rights correspondence was published in 2007. Acknowledging that Robinson often worked with a ghostwriter, even in his correspondence, one reviewer said that his voice was unmistakable: "He wrote like he played ball: with absolute confidence and a cutting aggression."

Robinson sent letters to presidents, both Republican and Democratic, until his death in 1972. He backed Eisenhower's vice president, Richard Nixon, in the 1960 election because, Robinson once said, Nixon had expressed sincere interest in honoring the Republicans' legacy as the party of Lincoln. A meeting with the Democratic candidate that year, meanwhile, had revealed John Kennedy to be poorly prepared.

Chock full o' Nuts
REG US PAT OFF

425 LEXINGTON AVENUE
New York 17, N. Y.

THE WHITE HOUSE
MAY 14 11 36 AM '58
RECEIVED

May 13, 1958

The President
The White House
Washington, D. C.

My dear Mr. President:

I was sitting in the audience at the Summit Meeting of Negro
Leaders yesterday when you said we must have patience. On
hearing you say this, I felt like standing up and saying, "Oh
no! Not again."

I respectfully remind you sir, that we have been the most
patient of all people. When you said we must have self-
respect, I wondered how we could have self-respect and remain patient considering the treatment accorded us through
the years.

17 million Negroes cannot do as you suggest and wait for the
hearts of men to change. We want to enjoy now the rights
that we feel we are entitled to as Americans. This we cannot do unless we pursue aggressively goals which all other
Americans achieved over 150 years ago.

As the chief executive of our nation, I respectfully suggest
that you unwittingly crush the spirit of freedom in Negroes
by constantly urging forbearance and give hope to those pro-
segregation leaders like Governor Faubus who would take
from us even those freedoms we now enjoy. Your own experience with Governor Faubus is proof enough that forbearance and not eventual integration is the goal the pro-
segregation leaders seek.

In my view, an unequivocal statement backed up by action
such as you demonstrated you could take last fall in deal-

The President   Page 2   May 13, 1958

ing with Governor Faubus if it became necessary, would let
it be known that America is determined to provide -- in the
near future -- for Negroes -- the freedoms we are entitled to under the constitution.

Respectfully yours,

Jackie Robinson

Jackie Robinson

JR:cc

In mid-1958, Eisenhower met with civil rights leaders at the White House. An Eisenhower aide characterized the session as a success but tempered his remarks with a reaction "even if success in this area is built on sand."

On either side of Eisenhower were Rev. Martin Luther King Jr. and A. Philip Randolph and at far right Roy Wilkins. Attorney General William Rogers stood next to Randolph.

THE WHITE HOUSE
WASHINGTON

June 24, 1958

MEMORANDUM FOR THE FILES

Subject: Meeting of Negro Leaders with the President - June 23, 1958

The President met with: Dr. Martin Luther King, Jr., President, Southern Christian Leadership Conference

A. Philip Randolph, International President, Brotherhood of Sleeping Car Porters

 Roy Wilkins, President, NAACP

Lester B. Granger, Executive Secretary, National Urban League

Also present were Attorney General Rogers, Frederic E. Morrow and myself.

After introductions, Mr. Randolph, as the spokesman, laid before the President the attached statement. He prefaced the written statement by commending the President strongly for the many efforts he has made to advance the political and economic status of the American Negro. He said that they would not be present at the meeting if they did not have the firm conviction that the President was a man of courage and integrity who had shown leadership and brought about accomplishment in this field. He spoke strongly and favorably about the President's action in the Little Rock episode. He then proceeded, beginning on page 4, to read the nine recommendations contained in the statement, including the closing paragraphs. Following this, he asked Dr. King to speak.

Dr. King said he wanted to comment about the first three of the recommendations and that, as a minister, he felt these recommendations were designed to help mobilize the emotions of the spirit which, in turn, would aid in the fight for abolishment of segregation. He said that a Presidential pronouncement as called for in the first recommendation would give a moral boost to the Nation. Speaking of the second

THE WHITE HOUSE
WASHINGTON

June 25, 1958

DE

MEMORANDUM FOR THE PRESIDENT

As an aftermath of your meeting with the Negro leaders, you may be interested in the following observations:

1. The Negro leaders were more than enthusiastic about their reception, the length of time granted for the meeting, the willingness to be heard and the willingness to speak, and the intense and sympathetic attention given them.

2. Immediately afterwards, they met with the press. Their accounts of the conference were faithful and honest. After much give-and-take, with repeated attempts to evoke criticism from the members of the group (particularly from Mr. Wilkins), a comment was made that they appeared to have been "brainwashed." Mr. Louis Lautier, only Negro member of the National Press Club, finally asked Mr. Wilkins (with some sarcasm), just what had occurred in the meeting which brought about the change in Mr. Wilkins' attitude from that of a month ago. Mr. Wilkins, visibly irritated, made no real response.

3. After a number of conversations with knowledgeable people, I am convinced that this meeting was an unqualified success -- even if success in this area is built on sand.

Rocco C. Siciliano

Atime of general peace for the country and economic well-being for many Americans, the 1950s are firmly linked in memory to the man who managed the country through the decade. Certain fashions and fads distinguished those years, from the Mamie Eisenhower hairdo to the Elvis Presley craze. Featured performers of the 1950s: children. Baby Boomer boys wanted to be frontiersman and cowboys and girls wanted to save Elvis from the Army and a severe haircut. Symbolizing it all: the man who gave his name to the era – Dwight Eisenhower.

Only five years after the first Scrabble sets were produced for the market, the game had taken the country by storm. Ike and Mamie played a round in 1954 at their farm near Gettysburg.

Lots of boys watched Roy Rogers on television and owned action figures of him and his palomino, Trigger, but few could have not only Rogers but also his wife and fellow performer, Dale Evans, over for his birthday party. The lucky boy was David Eisenhower, puffing up to blow out the candles on his cake as Roy and Dale looked on with David's parents, John and Barbara Jean, grandparents Dwight and Mamie, and great-grandmother Elvira Doud.

Just weeks after Eisenhower announced a two-year suspension of nuclear testing and in the middle of the Central High School integration drama in Little Rock, the president took a moment to consider another issue: corporal punishment.

The question: whether Jill Steinberg, a child in New York City, received too many spankings. That was Jill's claim in a letter she wrote the president – a letter that actually reached him.

In reply, the president was careful to stay clear of jurisdictional issues. He advised Jill to keep her distance from the family cookie jar and to see that her bedroom was squared away.

The result of the presidential advice? We don't know.

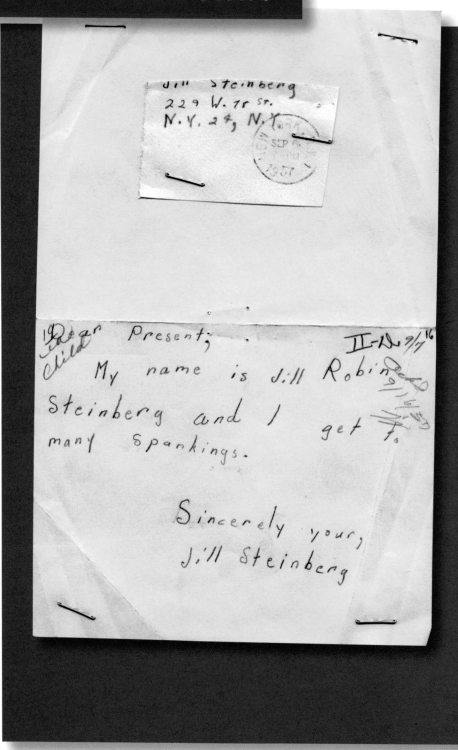

Checked by Kardex

Newport, Rhode Island,
September 21, 1957.

Dear Jill:

You have presented to me a different kind of
problem -- one that, I am afraid, would quite
mistakenly place me in the middle of a family
disagreement.

xPP259-B

If I may venture to advise you, I would suggest
that you have a little conversation with yourself
to discover the reasons why you are getting
these spankings. Possibly you have your hand
in the cookie jar too often or are careless about
keeping your room neat. Whatever the reason,
I believe that the best place to begin putting a
stop to these unpleasant experiences is to avoid
those things that little girls should not do. I am
quite certain that in this way the spankings will
be fewer and you will have just as much fun as
you are having now.

human interest
#

With best wishes,

Sincerely,

DWIGHT D. EISENHOWER

Robin
Jill Steinberg X
229 W. 78th Street
New York 24, New York

CROSS CARD FOR STAFF SECRETARY.'

"WE WILL JUST ABOUT DIE!"

Like a lot of young men in America in the 1950s, Elvis Presley was drafted into the Army. Unlike all the rest of the young men, he was a huge star. Before the rock 'n' roll icon was inducted in March 1958 his fans appealed to President Eisenhower. In their letters some worried about the singer's personal safety.

Others worried about his sideburns.

"He looks un-human without them," wrote one fan from Pennsylvania.

The president did not intervene. Presley joined the Army and received the obligatory, close G.I. haircut. Yet clearly he was not treated as just another draftee. A memo by an Army personnel officer, held today by the National Archives, suggests that the singer's military service would inspire other young men to volunteer, years before the volunteer military.

Presley served in a tank battalion in West Germany and left the Army in March 1960.

2/11/57

File

Dear Mr President,
           This letter concerns
Elvis Presley. My friends and
I are Elvis Presley fans, and
we don't want him to go
to the army. Because if
he is in the army, he will
have his sideburns cut off.
He looks unhuman without
them. When he is in the
army he won't be able
go on tours and sing
for his fans, and make
movies. If he is in
the army, he might
w have to go to war.

He might get killed. So
please don't make go to
the army.

      I would like you to
answer my letter, because
than I will know you
received this letter, and than
I will know what you
are going to do about it

P. S This is only   Sincerly yours,
a few of the names.   Dolores Castanzo
P. Morris   1122 10th Ave.
Marca Guilford   Beaver Falls
L. Schreangost   Pennsylvania
J. Jones,
L. Burns
D. Zarumberg
S. Panosida

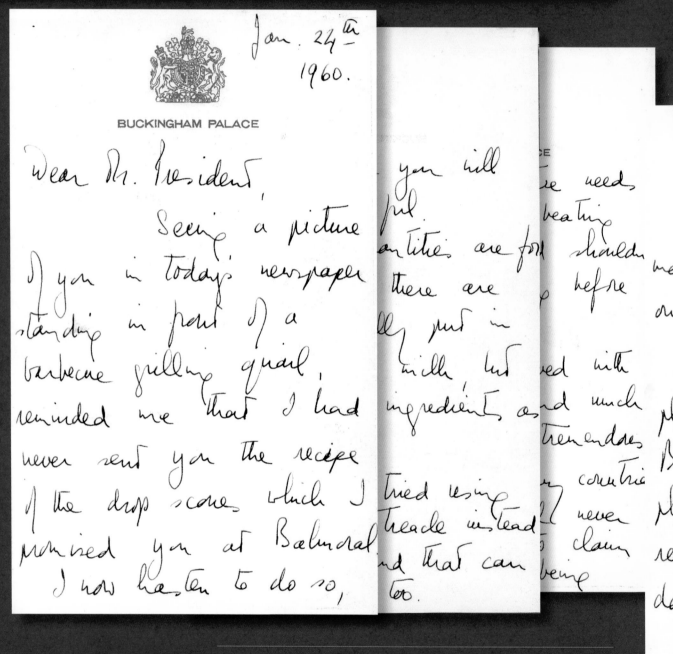

Jan. 24th 1960.

BUCKINGHAM PALACE

Dear Mr. President,

Seeing a picture of you in today's newspaper standing in front of a barbecue grilling quail, reminded me that I had never sent you the recipe of the drop scones which I promised you at Balmoral. I now hasten to do so,

Queen Elizabeth sent along a personal note and her recipe for scones to the president, who enjoyed cooking.

Date..

DROP SCONES

Ingredients

4 teacups flour

4 tablespoons caster sugar

2 teacups milk

2 whole eggs

2 teaspoons bi-carbonate soda

3 teaspoons cream of tartar

2 tablespoons melted butter

Beat eggs, sugar and about half the milk together, add flour, and mix well together adding remainder of milk as required, also bi-carbonate and cream of tartar, fold in the melted butter.

Enough for 16 people

7632 G.87 2M 2/55 H & S Gp. 902

to do too much on
ture Tour!

We remember with such
...e your visit to
...al, and I hope the
...aphs will be a
...er of the very happy
...ou spend with us.
...all good wishes to you
...s. Eisenhower.
...sincerely Elizabeth R

THE MAMIE LOOK

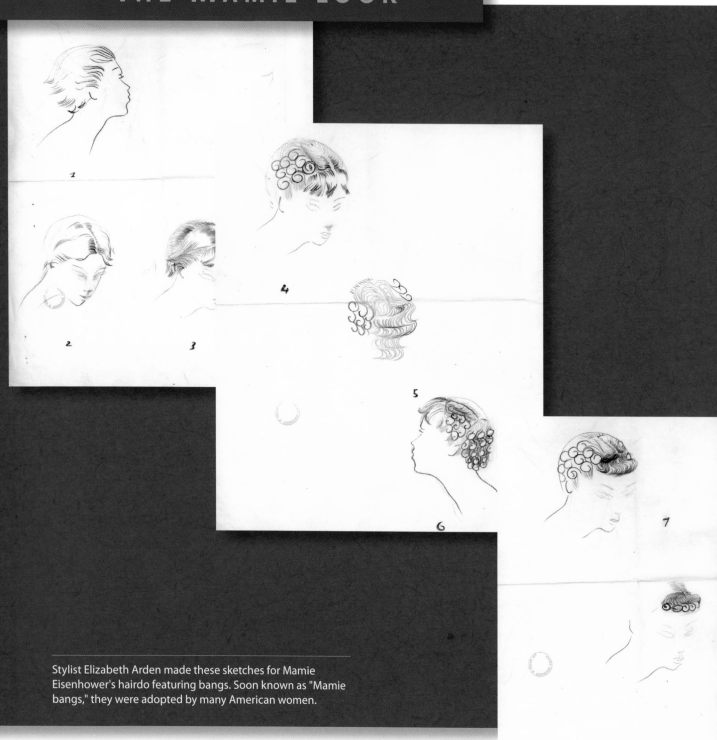

Stylist Elizabeth Arden made these sketches for Mamie Eisenhower's hairdo featuring bangs. Soon known as "Mamie bangs," they were adopted by many American women.

devant.

Above: The president with stars of stage and screen. From left, comedian Joe E. Brown, dancer Ray Bolger, singers Howard Keel, Connie Russell and Lena Horne, and pianist Liberace

Facing page: The Eisenhowers knew how to throw a party. In 1954, members of Eisenhower's 1915 graduating class at West Point, lined a White House stair case, everyone dressed in the height of 50s fashion.

In May 1959, about a month before mass murderer Charles Starkweather was scheduled to be executed in the Nebraska State Penitentiary, Caril Ann Fugate – who accompanied Starkweather on his rampage – played a desperate card.

She sent a telegram to President Eisenhower.

In it, she insisted that the teenaged Starkweather, whose 10 victims in 1958 included her own mother, stepfather and half-sister, had misled her and later lied about her participation in the killings.

"I know you are very busy," the 15-year-old Caril Ann told Eisenhower, "but please help me in any way you can."

Special counsel David Kendall responded promptly, saying the president had no jurisdiction in the case.

The Starkweather killings had shocked Americans. They resonated in American culture for years afterward, in films as well as in a song by Bruce Springsteen.

For her role, Fugate received a life sentence. She was paroled in 1976.

The White House
Washington

1959 MAY 21 PM 5 21

WA016 DL PD

WUX YORK NEBR MAY 21 215PMC

THE PRESIDENT

THE WHITE HOUSE

I AM NOW FIFTEEN YEARS OLD STOP ABOUT A YEAR AND ONE-HALF AGO ON A DAY WHEN I WAS IN PUBLIC SCHOOL NINETEEN YEAR OLD STARKWEATHER WHOM I HAD TOLD SEVERAL DAYS BEFORE IN FRONT OF MY MOTHER NEVER TO SEE ME AGAIN WENT INTO MY HOME AND KILLED MY TWO YEAR OLD BABY SISTER, MOTHER AND STEPFATHER. STOP STARKWEATHER FIRST CONFESSED I HAD NOTHING TO DO WITH HIS MURDERS WHICH IS TRUE STOP LATER HE

CHANGED HIS STORY AND SAID I HELPED HIM DO HIS MURDERS WHICH IS NOT TRUE STOP HE FORCED ME TO GO WITH HIM WHEN I GOT HOME FROM SCHOOL AGAINST MY WILL. STARKWEATHER WILL BE EXECUTED TOMORROW. STOP I HAVE BEEN DENIED BY GOVERNOR BROOKS A REQUEST TO SEE HIM AND SEE IF HE WILL TELL THE TRUTH IN FRONT OF A MINISTER OR SOME ONE ELSE WHO WOULD BE FAIR BEFORE HE IS EXECUTED. STOP I KNOW OF NO ONE ELSE TO TURN TO BECAUSE ALL OF MY FAMILY I WAS LIVING WITH HE KILLED STOP I KNOW YOU ARE VERY BUSY BUT PLEASE HELP ME IN ANY WAY YOU CAN. THANK YOU

CAROL ANN FUGATE.

GF 123-B, Nebraska

STANDARD FORM No. 14
APPROVED BY THE PRESIDENT
MARCH 10, 1926

TELEGRAM

OFFICIAL BUSINESS—GOVERNMENT RATES

FROM **David W. Kendall**

BUREAU

CHG. APPROPRIATION **Official**

RECEIVED
MAY 2 2 1959
CENTRAL FILES

10—1723   ☆ GPO:1952 O—998649

May 21, 1959

Miss Carol Ann Fugate
York
Nebraska

Charles

Because the Starkweather case is entirely a state matter, the President has
no jurisdiction or authority in any way to comply with your request.

David W. Kendall
Special Counsel to the President

Charles Starkweather
and Caril Ann Fugate in

ARE THEY OUT THERE?

Fueled by horror films, the threat of nuclear war, fear of Communists, rumor and sketchy reports, concerns that aliens from outer space were visiting earth sprang up after World War II and were going full steam by the 1950s. Stories circulated in earnest about an alien spacecraft that supposedly crashed in 1947 near Roswell Army Air Field in New Mexico. Since the early 1980s, requests from UFO buffs, or ufologists, have been a workplace reality for archivists at the Eisenhower Library. Inquiries were kept alive in the 1990s by the popularity of such films as "Independence Day" and television programs like "The X-Files."

Often, what ufologists want to know are the whereabouts of President Eisenhower on certain dates, and the authenticity of a briefing paper allegedly prepared for Eisenhower in November 1952, only days after his election as president. The document cited by ufologists appears to refer to a federal panel known as Majestic-12, or MJ-12, allegedly established by President Truman in 1947 to investigate a crash in Roswell. Archivists have never found the original document or any document even mentioning MJ-12.

Ufologists also wonder about the events of Feb. 20, 1954, when President Eisenhower was in Palm Springs, California, not far from Edwards Air Force Base. Some speculate that he traveled there that day either to meet aliens or to view their remains. Eisenhower's appointment books, however, indicate the president broke a cap on a tooth that night and visited the office of a local dentist, which opened especially for the presidential emergency.

The Eisenhower Library contains a few authentic documents about unexplained phenomena. Among them are a brief report by a scientific panel convened in January 1953 at the request of the director of central intelligence. The report, declassified in 1982, stated that there was no evidence that reports of flying saucers "constitute a direct physical threat to national security."

REPORT OF THE SCIENTIFIC PANEL
ON
UNIDENTIFIED FLYING OBJECTS

JAN 17 1953

1. Pursuant to the request of the Assistant Director for Scientific Intelligence, the undersigned Panel of Scientific Consultants has met to evaluate any possible threat to national security posed by Unidentified Flying Objects ("Flying Saucers"), and to make recommendations thereon. The Panel has received the evidence as presented by cognizant intelligence agencies, primarily the Air Technical Intelligence Center, and has reviewed a selection of the best documented incidents.

2. As a result of its considerations, the Panel concludes:

a. That the evidence presented on Unidentified Flying Objects shows no indication that these phenomena constitute a direct physical threat to national security.

We firmly believe that there is no residuum of cases which indicates phenomena which are attributable to foreign artifacts capable of hostile acts, and that there is no evidence that the phenomena indicate a need for the revision of current scientific concepts.

3. The Panel further concludes:

a. That the continued emphasis on the reporting of these phenomena does, in these parlous times, result in a threat to the orderly functioning of the protective organs of the body politic.

We cite as examples the clogging of channels of communication by irrelevant reports, the danger of being led by continued false alarms to ignore real

17436

A memo at the Eisenhower Library summarizes the report of former U.S. Sen. Richard Russell of Georgia, who, while on a trip to Russia in 1955, described seeing two "circular unconventional aircraft resembling flying discs or flying saucers."

Facing page: A New York man published a copy of an Air Force report on flying saucers, complete with illustrations.

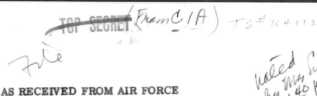

TOP SECRET (From CIA)   TS# 164112

FOLLOWING AS RECEIVED FROM AIR FORCE

FROM: USAIRA PRAGUE SIGNED RYAN

TO   :   CSAF WASH DC FOR DINTA

NR   :   C-103   NOFORN   October 13, 10 PM

Three reliable US observers, Senator Richard Russell, Lt. Col. E. U. Hathaway, Army, Mr. Ruben Efron, visited Prague 12-13 October. Arriving direct from Kiev, via Baku, Tiflis, Dnieper Petrovsk, Black Sea Area, and reported following to USAIRA and USARMA:

On 4 October 1955 at 1910 hours between Alyat Station and Adzhijabul (40 02 N-48 56 E) 10 minutes by rail after departing Alyat in Trans Caucasus Region, 2 mound (as received) and circular unconventional aircraft resembling flying discs or flying saucers were seen taking off almost vertically one minute apart. Disc aircraft ascended near dusk with outer surface revolving to right slowly and with 2 lights stationary on top near middle part. Sparks or flame seen coming from aircraft. No protrusions seen on aircraft which passed over observers' train. Both flying disc aircraft ascended relatively slowly to about 6,000 then speed increased sharply in horizontal flight both on northerly heading. Flying attitude of disc remained same during ascent as in cruise, like a discus in flight. Two operating searchlights pointing almost vertical seen near take-off area located about 1-2 miles south of railroad line. After sighting, Soviet train men became excited and lowered curtains and refused permission to look out windows. US observers firmly believe these unconventional aircraft are flying saucer or disc aircraft. USAIRA rates info B-2.

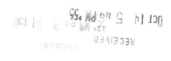

TOP SECRET

DECLASSIFIED
Authority MR 93-207#2
By ___ NLE Date 6/10/96

FLYING SAUCERS: An Analysis of the

AIR FORCE PROJECT BLUE BOOK SPECIAL REPORT NO. 14

by Dr. Leon Davidson

D-2

Publisher's Statement

The letter on page D-3 from Gen. Kinney indicates that the U.S. Air Force has not distributed the full 316-page Project Blue Book Special Report No. 14 because the cost would have been prohibitive. A letter from A.F. Secretary Donald A. Quarles, dated July 5, 1956, states: "It has been estimated that the cost of printing enough copies for distribution to the public through such outlets as libraries and academic institutions would be between $10 and $15 per copy."

This privately financed edition of the Blue Book report is being is-

Price

Case V (Serial 0565.00 to 0565.03)

A pilot and copilot were flying a DC-3 at 0340 hours on July 24, 1948, when they saw an object coming toward them. It passed to the right and slightly above them, at which time it went into a steep climb and was lost from sight in some clouds. Duration of the observation was about 10 seconds. One passenger was able to catch a flash of light as the object passed. The object seemed powered by rocket or jet motors shooting a trail of fire some 50 feet to the rear of the object. The object had no wings or other protrusion and had two rows of lighted windows.

Cockpit windshield?

Pilot

Case V

Windows with white light

A PASTIME AND A PASSION

To the young Dwight Eisenhower, successful professional baseball players represented a distant ideal. They occupied a niche apart from all other human beings.

"For half the year," he once wrote, "their names were featured in the daily paper. They made immense sums of money – three, four, five thousands dollars, and all for doing what was fun."

When as a boy in Abilene, Eisenhower indulged in fantasies of glory, it came in two forms: as a train engineer and as a baseball player. In his baseball reverie his favorite moment was "to set down the next three batters on nine pitches in the last half of the ninth, with the bases loaded (of course) to the thunderous applause of 500 spectators."

"Certainly," he added, "I never thought of myself or those about me as makers or participants in any other kind of history."

As a youth, Dwight Eisenhower was not only a fan. He also played the game – at Abilene High School and, according to biographer Carlo D'Este, for a semi-professional ball club in a nearby town under an assumed name. Perhaps Eisenhower hadn't wanted to lose his amateur status before leaving for West Point.

As president years later, Dwight Eisenhower sent birthday greetings to Honus Wagner. As a shortstop for the Pittsburgh Pirates, Wagner was one of the game's stars at the turn of the 20th century. In 1954, he turned 80 years old. The next year, Eisenhower sent a presidential message for the unveiling of a statue of Wagner near Forbes Field, the old ballpark in Pittsburgh. Presumably in thanks, Wagner sent an autographed baseball to the White House for Eisenhower.

In 1956, Eisenhower attended the first game of the World Series, but what for some presidents is a token gesture was not with Eisenhower. After the series, Eisenhower wrote Don Larsen of the New York Yankees, congratulating him on pitching a perfect game. *The Sporting News* obtained a copy of the letter and published it that November. Editors received a White House reprimand for printing a communication marked "private and personal."

Eisenhower also sent a sympathetic letter to Brooklyn Dodgers pitcher Don Newcombe, a Cy Young award winner that year who nevertheless pitched poorly against the Yankees in the World Series.

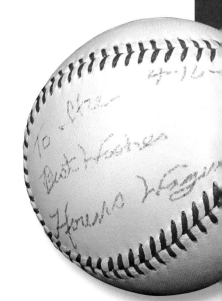

Left: The autographed baseball sent from Honus Wagner to Dwight Eisenhower. Wagner was a star player in Eisenhower's own baseball-playing years in the early 1900s at Abilene High School. Eisenhower is in the center of the front row, above.

Dear Mr. Eisenhower,
Here are three pictures of myself for you and your grandchildren. I am enjoying my stay in Dewey's State and I want to tell you that I hope to vote for you in 1956.
Sincerely Yours,

Denton T. (Cy) Young

Telephone 600

RICHARD TREADWAY, *Managing Dir.*   H. J. MERRICK, JR., *Manager*

Cooper Inn and Cottages
COOPERSTOWN, NEW YORK

Pitcher Cy Young, whose name is on the award given to baseball's finest pitchers each year, signed a postcard containing his Hall of Fame plaque and also a message on the back. "Dewey's state" refers to New York, home of Thomas Dewey, the GOP presidential candidate in 1944 and 1948.

First-pitch duties at Griffith Stadium in Washington. With opening day of the major-league baseball season came an invitation from the Washington Senators to toss the ceremonial first pitch. Among the notables looking on when the Senators played the Yankees in 1953, above, were Casey Stengel in his New York uniform and Senate Minority Leader Lyndon B. Johnson, to Eisenhower's right. When the Red Sox opened the Senators' season in 1960, right, Vice President Richard Nixon was among the celebrities. He was seated to the president's right. Between them was Secretary of State Christian Herter.

New York Yankees

EXECUTIVE OFFICES • 745 FIFTH AVENUE
NEW YORK 22, N. Y. • PLAZA 9-5300

BUSINESS AND TICKET OFFICES • YANKEE STADIUM
BRONX 51, N. Y. • CYPRESS 3-4300

Concourse Plaza Hotel
The Bronx, N.Y.

October 23, 1956

Hon. Dwight D. Eisenhower
The White House
Washington, D. C.

Dear Mr. President:

I can't begin to tell you how much I appreciated your recent letter. And, if anyone was to ask me now what is the greatest thrill I've ever experienced, I'd certainly find it difficult trying to decide between the no-hitter and the congratulatory note I received from you.

My only regret is that I didn't have the privilege of pitching my perfect game with you on hand. I guess that really would have topped everything!

My deepest thanks again and warmest wishes that you and your family enjoy continued good health and a long and successful stay in the White House.

With kindest personal regards, I am

Most sincerely,

Don Larsen

Don Larsen

Two pitchers who played in the 1956 World Series received notes from the president and sent him thanks. Don Larsen of the New York Yankees, above, pitched a perfect game in the series; no runner even reached first base. Don Newcombe of the Brooklyn Dodgers, right, wasn't as fortunate.

CABLE ADDRESS "IMPHO TOKYO"

Imperial Hotel

Tokyo

Oct. 11, 1956

Dear Sir,

Just a line to let you know that I received your very nice letter. I don't think you'll ever know what it has done for my confidence, which was at a very low ebb. I was very pleased to learn that you were pulling for the Dodgers and me personally and I'm very sorry that I didn't do better, and through your letter I think I understand more clearly about the bad breaks in sports. With kindest personal regards I remain

Sincerely

Don Newcombe

BABE RUTH
NEW YORK

July 8, 1948

General Dwight D. Eisenhower,
President, Columbia University,
116th Street and Broadway,
New York, New York.

Dear General Eisenhower:

It would make me very
happy if you and Mrs. Eisenhower would be my
guests at the Premiere of the motion picture,
The Babe Ruth Story, on Monday evening, July
26th, at the Astor Theatre.

The proceeds of this per-
formance, as well as of Premieres in other
cities throughout the country, will go to the
Babe Ruth Foundation, which will help the "Kids
of America".

I do hope that you will be
able to be with me.

Sincerely,

Babe Ruth

Room 937,
Memorial Hospital
444 East 68th Street,
New York, N. Y.

From his hospital room, a dying Babe Ruth invited the
Eisenhowers to the opening of a movie about Ruth's life.

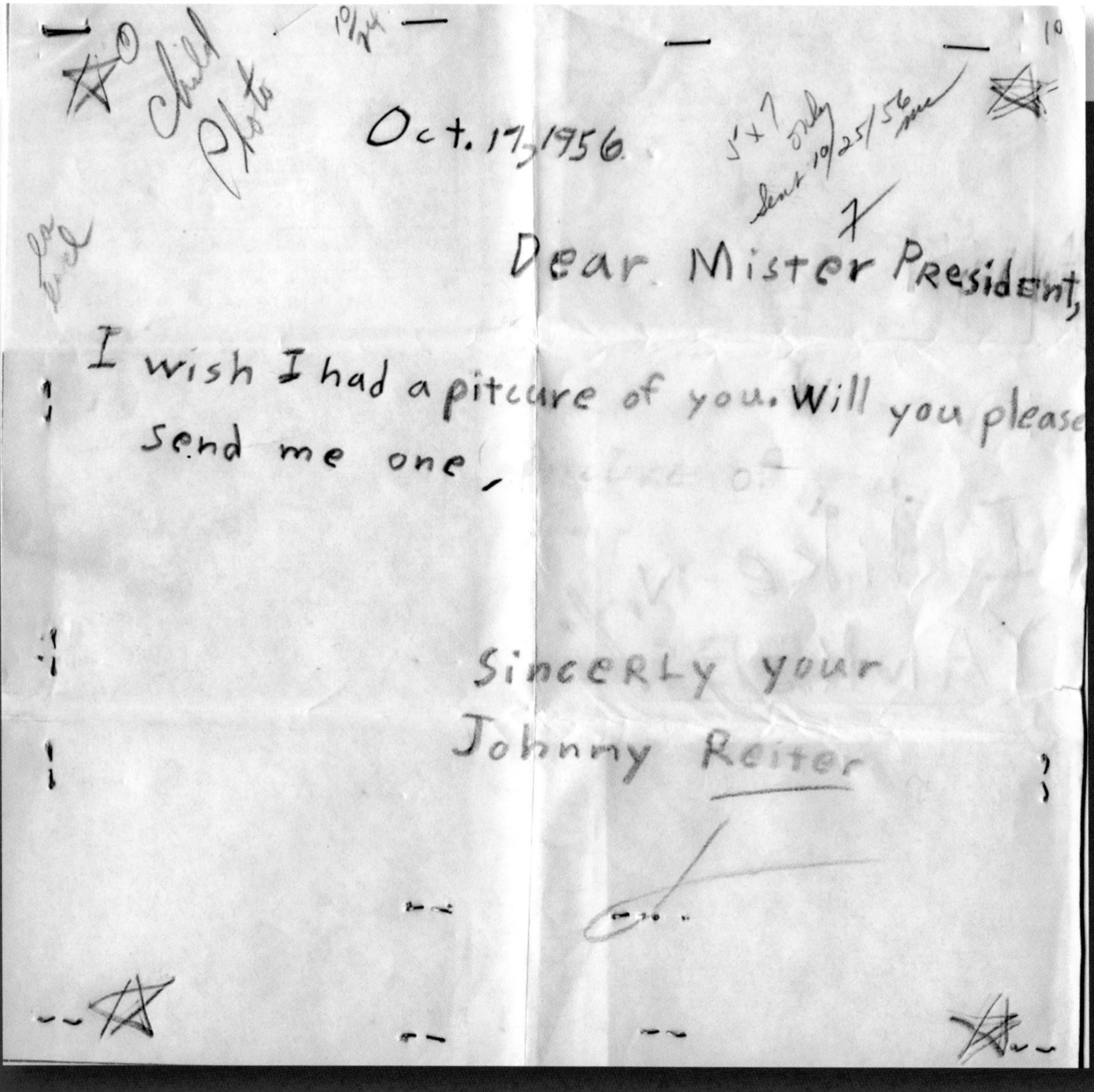

Oct. 17, 1956

Dear Mister President,

I wish I had a pitcure of you. Will you please send me one,

Sincerly your
Johnny Reiter

One young baseball fan who wanted a picture of the president sent along baseball cards of his favorite players – all New York Yankees.

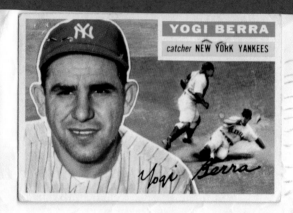

YOGI BERRA
catcher NEW YORK YANKEES

Yogi Berra

HANK BAUER
outfield NEW YORK YANKEES

Hank Bauer

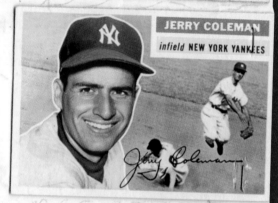

JERRY COLEMAN
infield NEW YORK YANKEES

Jerry Coleman

I like N.Y.
YANKEES.

"WHITEY" FORD
pitcher NEW YORK YANKEES

Edward Ford

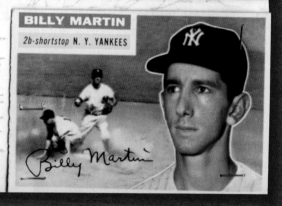

BILLY MARTIN
2b-shortstop N. Y. YANKEES

Billy Martin

ON THE BEACH

In 1983, Secretary of State George Schultz appeared on network television to re-assure Americans that nuclear annihilation was not imminent. The occasion was the network television broadcast of "The Day After," a film showing the effects of a nuclear war on American life. At least one television commentator found it remarkable that anyone with high cabinet rank felt compelled to comment on a movie.

A Cabinet-level response to Hollywood, however, was not unprecedented.

In 1959, the Eisenhower Cabinet produced a paper recommending specific administration responses to the new film "On the Beach," which depicted the apparent end of life on Earth from radiation fallout after a nuclear war. The movie featured A-list stars as Gregory Peck, Ava Gardner, Fred Astaire and Anthony Perkins. In the film, the characters they played were doomed.

The Cabinet paper, noting that "On the Beach" was to premiere in December not only in the United States but also in major cities around the world, asked overseas representatives of the State Department and United States Information Agency to report press and public reaction by telegram.

"Our attitude should be one of matter-of-fact interest, showing no special concern," it cautioned. The paper pointed out what federal officials considered scientific errors in the script – "fallout radiation diminishes so rapidly with time and distance" – yet counseled that public criticism of the movie would be counter-productive.

Rather, U.S. representatives should talk up the Eisenhower administration's support for "safe-guarded disarmament measures." Mention ongoing disarmament negotiations, the paper suggested, and include the sentiment that "with patience and persistence, real progress is attainable…."

If American personnel overseas got questions about the effects of nuclear fallout, the paper alerted them to a pamphlet sent by air-pouch two months before, entitled "Biological and Environmental Effects of Nuclear War."

"Its strong emotional appeal for banning nuclear weapons could conceivably lead audiences to think in terms of radical solutions...."

CONFIDENTIAL

CABINET PAPER—PRIVILEGED

Property of the White House—For Authorized Persons Only

OUTGOING   U. S. INFORMATION AGENCY
MESSAGE
VIA POUCH

INFOGUIDE 60-24 DECEMBER 4, 1959
           USIA CIRCULAR
SENT TO: JOINT USIA-STATE   PRIORITY

INFOGUIDE: "On the Beach"

"On the Beach," a major Hollywood treatment of nuclear war, will be simultaneously premiered in the US and fifteen other countries on December 17. The premieres are being heralded with extensive publicity and will probably attract wider-than-usual audiences. Moreover, the controversial aspects of the film may well result in additional publicity. (For list of premiere cities and synopsis of film, see "BACKGROUND" at end of this message). Posts are requested to report initial press and public reaction to the film by telegram.

The film, which is highly fictionalized and contains scientific inaccuracies, raises once again the general question of what is to be done about nuclear weapons. Its strong emotional appeal for banning nuclear weapons could conceivably lead audiences to think in terms of radical solutions to the problem rather than in terms of practical safeguarded disarmament measures. To a limited extent, however, it may offer opportunities to turn this emotional response into intellectual support of our quest for safeguarded disarmament.

GUIDANCE:

Our attitude should be one of matter-of-fact interest, showing no special concern; it should reflect the fact that the issues raised by the film are not new, but have been articulated by thoughtful people over more than a decade. We should refrain from public criticism of the film, which would be counter-productive; on the other hand, we should carefully avoid any implications of U. S. government approval. We should, however, be ready to discuss the film in private conversation, and give a reasoned opinion on it when appropriate. In this connection, officers who may expect to be discussing the film should not hesitate to see it if this can be done without implying approval.

While recognizing that little can be done to affect the film's impact on foreign audiences, we believe the following points, which bear on this question and certain constructive answers to it, may be useful as appropriate in private discussions with government officials or opinion leaders:

1. Though fictional from the scientific viewpoint (see point 2) the film will take most viewers through a strong emotional experience. Actually, the greatest impact of the film for thinking people should be to underline once more the vital importance of achieving safeguarded disarmament.

In this connection these special points may be noted:

a. To avoid a catastrophic war, the U.S. since 1945 has placed special emphasis on achieving a safeguarded disarmament agreement covering both nuclear and conventional arms. This effort to do something about the threat of accumulating armament holds new promise of bearing fruit. The Geneva test ban

CABINET PAPER—PRIVILEGED

Property of the White House—For Authorized Persons Only

negotiations and the scheduled resumption of general disarmament negotiations in 1960 suggest that with patience and persistence, real progress is attainable;

b. Until safeguarded disarmament is achieved, the US and its allies must maintain armed strength to deter aggression and for self-protection if conflict should break out;

c. Disarmament is indivisible -- must be pursued both for nuclear and conventional weapons -- since to reduce nuclear arms alone would be to renounce the free world's counterweight against superior Soviet-bloc conventional forces;

d. War itself is the real evil, not any particular weapon. Conventional weapons kill just as effectively as nuclear weapons; morally there is no distinction.

2. It will be unfortunate if the scientific inaccuracies of the film mislead people and drive them to pressure for ban-the-bomb-type solutions to the nuclear weapons problem.

The two basic flaws in the film's treatment of the scientific aspects of fallout may be noted:

a. Fallout radiation diminishes so rapidly with time and distance from the source that it would be inconceivable for people a long distance away to be killed by fallout from a nuclear conflict -- even assuming that maximum possible bombs were dropped. For example, no one in the southern hemisphere would be killed, or probably even made sick, by a nuclear war as far away as the northern hemisphere. Effect of fallout radiation from a nuclear conflict would be confined to countries directly attacked or those close by. Thus, unless active hostilities were to spread to every part of the globe, a nuclear conflict would not mean "the end of the world".

b. The assumption that nothing can be done to protect people from fallout is wrong and is highly misleading. Much could and would be done. Civil defense tests carried out under actual nuclear bomb explosion conditions have amply proved that effective measures can be taken against fallout (chiefly shelters and decontamination). As far away as another hemisphere, however, if any protection at all were needed an ordinary basement would suffice.

(NOTE: The latest authoritative statement of these points is contained in the June 1959 hearings of the Radiation Subcommittee of the Joint Committee on Atomic Energy of the U.S. Congress, which was airpouched to USIS posts September 20 in a pamphlet entitled "Biological and Environmental Effects of Nuclear War". See pages 8 and 53.)

3. The film grossly misconstrues the basic nature of man. The resort to mass suicide is not only unnecessary but wholly fatalistic, misinterpreting the vitality of the human spirit. It is inconceivable that even in the event of a nuclear war, mankind would not have the strength and ingenuity to take all possible steps toward self-preservation.

1. World premiere

Advance promotion for "On the Beach" has been on an unprecedented scale, and has included extensive advance showings to film critics, government agencies and other groups in the US and abroad. The simultaneous world premiere December 17 includes four cities in the US (New York, Chicago, Los Angeles and Washington) and fifteen cities in other countries, as follows: Amsterdam, Berlin, Caracas, Johannesburg, Lima, London, Madrid, Melbourne, Moscow, Paris, Rome, Stockholm, Tokyo, Toronto and Zurich. The Moscow premiere was an added starter, announced November 29.

2. Synopsis

"On the Beach", produced by Stanley Kramer and distributed by United Artists, follows closely the 1957 novel of the same name by Nevile Shute.

The story takes place in 1964, following a major nuclear war which is frequently mentioned but never specifically described. The action is mainly in Australia, which is pictured as the last place in the world where life still goes on, because the fallout has not reached there yet. The characters in the film are gripped by a sense of impending doom, since it is predicted the fallout will arrive in Australia in five months. Daily life consists largely of attempts at diversion through preoccupation with business-as-usual, excessive drinking, etc. The chief actors are Gregory Peck, Ava Gardner, and Fred Astaire.

Action opens as the sole surviving U.S. naval vessel, a submarine, makes its way to Australia. The Australian government assigns the captain to take his ship and crew on an inspection tour to check radioactivity levels. The ship calls at San Francisco, which is intact but completely empty of people as seen through the periscope. A visit is then made to a similarly deserted oil refinery near San Diego to check the source of a mysterious, incomprehensible radio signal; a plastic-suited investigator from the ship finds a transmitter key being randomly tapped by a coke bottle caught in the blowing drawstring of a window shade.

On the submarine's return to Australia, people are beginning to get sick from fallout. There is no discussion of preventive measures; everyone implicitly agrees that there is nothing to be done. The people queue up for suicide pills, to be used when the time comes. A shot of people gathered for a revivalist meeting in a town square focusses on a banner reading: "Brother, there is still time..." The submarine crew decides to return to the U.S. to die. The picture ends with a reprise of the town square, this time with no people, and a final shot of the banner: "Brother, there is still time..."

SENT TO:

AMSTERDAM (FROM HERTER)		
BERLIN	BERN	STOCKHOLM
BONN	CARACAS	TOKYO
CANBERRA	HAGUE	TORONTO (FROM HERTER)
JOHANNESBURG	LIMA	ZURICH (FROM HERTER)
LONDON	MADRID	
MELBOURNE HERTER	PARIS	RPT INFO:
MOSCOW (FROM DILLON)	PRETORIA	ALL OTHER USIS
OTTAWA	ROME	PRINCIPAL POSTS

CABINET PAPER   ALLEN

SPACE

When astronaut Alan Shepard became the first American astronaut launched into space in 1961, it was President John Kennedy who honored him at the White House. In 1969, when astronauts set foot on the moon, it was President Richard Nixon who called to congratulate them.

Yet the Space Age began in America in the 1950s under President Eisenhower. Research into rocketry and orbital satellites was under way throughout the decade and received a massive boost in late 1957, when the Soviet Union successfully launched the first unmanned earth satellite, Sputnik.

Holding a U.S. flag carried into space, the president stood next to a capsule retrieved from Discoverer XIII and brought to the White House in August 1960.

In September 1960 the George C. Marshall Space Flight Center was dedicated in Huntsville, Alabama. Scientist Wernher von Braun showed President Eisenhower a display about the Atlas rocket.

MOSCOW STEALS A MARCH

For many Americans, the world changed on October 4, 1957.

That's when news broke that the Soviet Union had launched a 184-pound artificial satellite and successfully placed it in orbit. The United States had tried the same thing, but failed. Many Americans went to their backyards at night, looking up and trying to spot Sputnik in the skies. Shortwave radio operators picked up Sputnik's beeping transmissions.

Time magazine referred to the "Red Moon over the U.S."

Future president Lyndon Johnson, then Senate majority leader, would later remark how the night sky in Texas, always a familiar part of his life, "seemed almost alien" after Sputnik.

The Soviet satellite, wrote historian Stephen Ambrose, "swept away certain basic American assumptions and caused a crisis in self-confidence."

When President Eisenhower walked into his press conference on Oct. 9, 1957, a reporter opened the proceedings with a reference to Sputnik and said:

"I ask you, sir, what are going to do about it?"

Eisenhower apparently hadn't anticipated the extent of the nation's reaction.

"Most surprising of all," Eisenhower wrote in a memoir, "was the intensity of the public concern."

Yet it was not surprising that the Soviet success, occurring as it had in a Cold War climate, would prompt fear among many Americans. If the Soviets could launch a successful satellite, what else could they do?

Only the day before, at a White House cabinet meeting, the president and others had heard Donald Quarles, assistant secretary of defense, estimate that the thrust of the rocket used to launch Sputnik was more powerful than any rocket available to the United States.

At the same meeting, however, Quarles also said that the Soviets – whatever their propaganda triumph – had done the United States a favor.

Because their satellite was the first to fly around the world and all its sovereign countries, the launch had established an international protocol for orbital space, one that shrugged aside international borders. Basically, Sputnik's orbit made the case that outer space was free to all. That was important because the United States was considering proposals for reconnaissance satellites.

"We believe that we can get a great deal more information out of free use of orbital space than they can," the cabinet minutes read.

Additionally, the United States and the Soviet Union were two of 40 nations whose scientists were participating in the International Geophysical Year, a global cooperative study. In fact, Soviet representatives had been open with many details of its satellite program. Yet that

Conference in the President's Office, 8:30 a.m., Oct. 8, 1957. Present:
The President, Quarles, Waterman, Holaday, Hagen, Adams, Persons,
Hagerty, Harlow, Pyle, Goodpastor, Cutler.

1. Quarles presented and explained a memorandum on the Earth
Satellite, Oct. 7, 1957 (copy filed with NSC).

2. The President decided not to shift from the present orderly
procedure to produce an Earth Satellite. It is understood that
Mr. Holaday will counsel with the Army. Quarles suggested that for an
additional $13 million the Army could provide a rocket capable of
orbiting the Satellite about one month ahead of the proposed orbiting
in March, 1958 (using Navy rocketry).

3. The Department of Defense will issue a statement along the
lines presented by Quarles and attached to the above-mentioned memorandum (detached and given to Hagerty).

4. The President made these guiding points:

 a. The U. S. determined to make the Satellite a scientific
 project and to keep it free from military weaponry to the

 b. No pressure or priority was exerted by the U.S. on timing,
 so long as the Satellite would be orbited during the
 IGY 1957-1958.

 c. The U.S. Satellite program was intended to meet scientific
 requirements with a view toward permitting all scientists
 to share in information which the U.S. might eventually
 acquire.

5. Quarles made the important point that the Russians having been
the first with their Satellite to overfly **all** countries, they have
thereby established the international characteristic of orbital space.
We believe that we can get a great deal more information out of free use
of orbital space than they can.

6. Quarles briefly described the Air Reconnaissance Satellite. We
can direct its initial orbit. It will orbit the world in about 1 hour
and 36 minutes. As the Earth is constantly orbiting itself, a new Earth
surface will be presented each time of orbit to the Air Reconnaissance
Satellite.

7. Apparently the thrust of the rocket used by the Russians to put
up their Satellite was around 200,000. The thrust of our rockets runs
from 27,000 (Redstone) up to 150,000 at present. It is believed that
the Russian rocket was the one used in their August rocket tests.
Quarles pointed out that the Army had sent up a rocket within a year
6/700 miles in the air. Its speed was much lower than the speed of the
rocket used by the Russians, - probably mach 12 at the peak, with a very
much lower speed at the top of the trajectory.

- 1 -

, the Russians have offered to
 in the next Satellite launched.
 blem for us as we do not think
 ery delicate material which we
 arently, our scientists believe
 r more crude and less instrumented

 ave today for his press conference

 was being taken by the U. S. in
 es beginning in 1953?

 first scientific committee set

 the Killian Committee's consideration of guided missiles.

 (4) What were the priorities for guided missiles and the
 date of establishment for the priorities?

 (5) As to the Earth Satellite:

 a. The date and nature of Killian Committee consideration?
 b. What were the priorities for the Earth Satellite and
 the date of establishment of such priorities?

 (6) What were the estimated costs for the Earth Satellite
 program and the dates of establishing those costs? (The
 President's recollection was that the final cost estimated
 was $110 million, with a possibility of going to
 $150 million, the increase being due largely to increased
 instrumentation and reserves for contingencies; it being
 understood that an increase up to $150 million would
 require further consideration by the President).

Notes from a White House strategy session.

subtle point was lost in a new rush to respond.

Meanwhile, propaganda efforts were under way to diminish the Soviet scientific achievement. A memo to Robert Cutler, an Eisenhower adviser, suggested that the United States coordinate a psychological campaign to combat "the present Soviet advantages."

The program would include deliberately over-playing Soviet capabilities in science and space "so that failure to perform would make the public think they are not as good as now appears."

On November 3, 1957, the Soviet Union launched a second satellite, this one carrying a dog. The spacecraft weighed 1,120 pounds.

On January 31, 1958, American scientists launched their own satellite. Named Explorer, it weighed 30 pounds.

Facing page: A memo from one administrative adviser suggested responses to Sputnik

October 10, 1957

MEMORANDUM TO MR. CUTLER

SUBJECT: Soviet Earth Satellite

1.   The OCB luncheon meeting yesterday and the NSC meeting this morning clearly indicate to me the need for intensive and immediate coordination in two fields:

a.   A psychological campaign, directed towards domestic and foreign opinion, to combat the present Soviet advantages: to include, for example, a deliberate overplaying of Russian capabilities so that failure to perform would make the public think they are not as good as now appears. I notice the British have already started this by announcing the next satellite would be launched in November, which announcement the Russians have denied; and

b.   The preparation, either for use as Mr. Stassen suggested or for use in Congress as the Vice President suggested, or both, of a coordinated brief showing, among other things and to the extent permitted by security, our knowledge of Soviet missile progress and our own progress to date.

2.   The OCB staff is now preparing terms of reference for a special working group on this subject, which it is planned to present to the Board next Wednesday. (See attached draft.)

3.   I also think that this morning's discussion clearly indicates the need for an extremely firm directive to the Defense Department if we are to avoid a Manhattan Project or a crash program with extremely heavy expenses.

4.   I believe that Messrs. Herter and Dulles are worried about the People-to-People program. Do you think we should ask for more details as to the Committee's use of its present name and the use of the name itself by individuals and groups traveling abroad.

~~TOP SECRET~~   F. M. Dearborn, Jr.

WA012 NL PD

TUCSON ARIZ NOV 3   1957 NOV 4   AM 6 56

THE PRESIDENT

   THE WHITE HOUSE

DEAR IKE, WE OF THE UPSILON ALPHA CHAPTER OF PHI GAMMA

DELTA AT THE UNIVERSITY OF ARIZONA WISH TO DONATE THE

SERVICES OF OUR DOG COSMO FOR SPACE TRAVEL IN THE UNITED

STATES OF AMERICA'S FIRST SATELLITE (IKENIK)

   THE FIJIS.

When the Soviet Union launched its much-publicized second satellite containing a dog, Laika, the White House began received telegrams from Americans offering their animals for a trip in space. Most were offered tongue in cheek.

Facing page: A Philadelphian had a serious suggestion, to consider the well-being of the passenger – animal or human – before launching it into space. The concern was well-founded. The Soviets had made no provision for the dog to return safely. It died several days into the mission.

WESTERN UNION
PRESS MESSAGE

EDITION
AM ——— PM
DEAD LINE

W. P. MARSHALL, PRESIDENT

1595 (R-11-52)
CHECK
RECEIVED
FEB 18 958
TIME FILED
CENTRAL FILES

AZA14 LONG DL PD ROANOKE VIR FEB 1 1243PME

G.F.
145-F

HON DWIGHT D EISENHOWER

     THE LITTLE WHITE HOUSE AUGUSTA GA

THE GROUND HOG CLUB OF AMERICA NO 1' INC ROANOKE VIRGINIA,

GROUND HOG CAPITOL OF THE UNIVERSE GATHERED IN ANNUAL SESSION

OF ITS BOARD OF DIRECTORS, HAS ADOPTED THE FOLLOWING RESOLUTION.

BE IT RESOLVED:

     THAT THE BOARD EXTEND ITS HEARTIEST CONGRATULATIONS AND

FELICITATIONS TO THE COMMANDER-IN-CHIEF OF OUR ARMED FORCES, AND TO

THOSE REDOUBTABLE MEN WHO HAVE SUCCESSFULLY LAUNCHED INTO THE

WORLD ORBIT, THE FIRST AMERICAN SATELLITE.

     BE IT FURTHER RESOLVED THAT IT IS THE FERVENT PRAYER,

SPEAKING FOR ALL AMERICANS, THAT THIS SUCCESSFUL LAUNCHING WILL BE

ONE TO INSURE AND GUARANTEE UNIVERSAL PEACE.

     BE IT FURTHER RESOLVED THAT IF THE ARMED FORCES DEEM IT

NECESSARY TO USE AN ANIMAL IN THE NEXT LAUNCHING OF AN EXPERIMENTAL

SATELLITE, IT IS RESPECTFULLY URGED THAT THE TRADITIONAL WEATHER

OBSERVER OF ALL TIMES, THE RELIABLE GROUND HOG, BE SELECTED FOR

THIS OUTER SPACE MISSION

     H T "JUBAL" ANGELL PRESIDENT GROUND HOG CLUB OF AMERICA

NO 1 INC

WA014 NL PD

PHILADELPHIA PENN NOV 3

THE PRESIDENT

  THE WHITEHOUSE

UNLESS THE RUSSIAN SCIENTISTS CAN SUCCEED IN

BRINGING DOWN THE DOG THEY SENT UP INTO OUTER

SPACE UNHARMED I THINK THEY SHOULD BE EXPELLED

FROM FURTHER FELLOWSHIP IN THE GEOPHYSICAL YEAR

PARTICIPATIONS FOR THEIR PREMATURE EXPERIMENT

SURELY SENSE WOULD DICTATE FIRST TO ATTEMPT TO

BRING A SATELLITE DOWN SAFELY BEFORE INVADING OUR

LIVES AND THE SKY IN A DEMONSTRATION THAT MUST

SICKEN ANY THINKING PERSON IN THE NAME OF GOD MR

PRESIDENT LET US NOT OURSELVES EXPERIMENT IN THIS

FASHION LEST EVERY HUMANE MEMBER OF THE RACE FIND

THE WORLD AN ALTOGETHER UNFIT PLACE TO LIVE IN

  MARION CLARKE 603 LOVE LANE WYNNEWOOD PENN.

In 1958 the National Aeronautics and Space Administration was born after President Eisenhower and Senate Majority Leader Lyndon Johnson came to terms on the extent of its authority.

In an off-the-record meeting that year, the two agreed that NASA would operate with an advisory body that included the president and also three members outside the federal government. NASA got control of all space activities except those the President determined primarily for national defense.

Yet Eisenhower's real wish was for U.S. space activities to come under the Pentagon. He wanted emphasis on missiles, not satellites, and apparently grumbled to Vice President Richard Nixon about the creation of a civilian agency. Eisenhower, wrote historian Stephan Ambrose, did not want the United States to be part of any "pathetic race" that involved scientific endeavors in outer space.

Nevertheless, the Space Age – and the Space Race – had begun.

85TH CONGRESS
2D SESSION

H. R. 12575

IN THE HOUSE OF REPRESENTATIVES

MAY 20, 1958

Mr. McCormack introduced the following bill; which was referred to the Select Committee on Astronautics and Space Exploration

A BILL

To provide for research into problems of flight within and outside the earth's atmosphere, and for other purposes.

1   *Be it enacted by the Senate and House of Representa-*

2   *tives of the United States of America in Congress assembled,*

3   TITLE I—SHORT TITLE AND DECLARATION OF

4   POLICY

5   SHORT TITLE

6   SEC. 101. This Act may be cited as the "National

7   Aeronautics and Outer Space Act of 1958".

8   DECLARATION OF POLICY AND PURPOSE

9   SEC. 102. (a) It is the policy of the United States

10   that—

I

EARLIEST POSSIBLE TIME PERIODS OF VARIOUS
SOVIET AND U. S. ACCOMPLISHMENTS IN OUTER SPACE

(NOTE: Generally, Soviet vehicles will be of substantially greater
orbital payloads than U. S. vehicles. It should be noted,
however, that the comparative capabilities of the United
States and the USSR should not be measured by orbital payloads alone. The United States is estimated to be consid-
erably ahead of the USSR in miniaturization of missile and
satellite components, and therefore the effectiveness of
U. S. satellites on a "per pound in orbit" basis is estimated to be greater than that of the USSR.)

		SOVIET[a]	U. S.[b]
1.	Scientific Earth Satellites (IGY Commitment)	1957-58	1958
2.	Reconnaissance Satellites[c]	1958-59	1959-61
3.	Recoverable Aeromedical Satellites	1958-59	1959
4.	Exploratory Lunar Probes or Lunar Satellites	1958-59	1958-59
5.	"Soft" Lunar Landing	1959-60	Early 1960
6.	Communications Satellites	---	1959-60
7.	Manned Recoverable Satellites		
	a. Capsule-type Satellites	1959-60[d]	(1960-63
	b. Glide-type Vehicles	1960-61	(
8.	Mars Probe	Aug. 1958[e]	Oct. 1960
9.	Venus Probe	June 1959[e]	Jan. 1961
10.	25,000-pound Satellite -- manned	1961-62	After 1965
11.	Manned Circumlunar Flight	1961-62	1962-64
12.	Manned Lunar Landing	After 1965	1968

a/ Estimate by the Guided Missile Intelligence Committee (GMIC) of the
IAC as of June 3, 1958.
b/ Source: Department of Defense, June 4, 1958.
c/ Defense Comment: (See Annex B for test reconnaissance satellites.)
The United States plans to launch a complete operational reconnaissance
satellite of approximately 3,000 pounds in late 1959. During the same
time period the USSR is estimated to be capable of launching a
4-5,000 pound reconnaissance satellite.
d/ The Joint Staff member of GMIC reserves his position on the date 1959.
e/ The Soviets most likely would attempt probes when Venus and Mars are in
their most favorable conjunction with the earth for such an undertaking.

A White House estimate of the prospects for U.S. vs. Soviet
space successes in the decade to come.

IMMEDIATE RELEASE   December 19, 1958

James C. Hagerty, Press Secretary to the President

P.P.F.
20-X-142

THE WHITE HOUSE

TEXT OF THE MESSAGE BY THE PRESIDENT,
RELAYED FROM THE SATELLITE "SCORE"
AND RECEIVED AT CAPE CANAVERAL, FRIDAY
AFTERNOON, DECEMBER 19, 1958

This is the President of the United States speaking.

Through the marvels of scientific advance my voice is

coming to you from a satellite circling in outer space.

My message is a simple one. Through this unique means

I convey to you and to all mankind America's wish for

peace on earth and good will toward men everywhere.

# # # # # # # # # # #

President Eisenhower recorded a message of peace broadcast
from a satellite in the weeks before Christmas 1958.

Facing page: Even in the late 1950s, Americans disagreed over
the need for a space program.

AMEDIC
SURGICAL COMPANY

1501 N. W. 10TH AVENUE

Miami 36, Florida

acke 2/6/59 flg

15

January 10, 1959

President Dwight D. Eisenhower
The White House
Washington 25, D. C.

Dear Sir:

I may not be too smart, but I don't understand why in the world anyone would want to live
on the moon and what good it will do for us to
learn if there is anyone living on the moon or
on the sun, or any of the other planets, insofar
as that is concerned.

It seems a shame to spend the billions of
dollars that is being spent to explore outer
space.

missiles x GF150-J-1

To expend money for the rockets which are
a defense measure is an entirely different thing,
and I certainly want to enter my protest, with I
am sure, many others.

Let the Russians reach the moon and stay there,
if they want to.

In a cartoon in the recent issue of the Miami
Daily News, by Ernest Sanders, a prayer was given,
which was:

SURGEON'S INSTRUMENTS
PHYSICIANS AND HOSPITAL
EQUIPMENT AND SUPPLIES
PHONE FR 9-4535

Serving the Medical Profession Since 1926

COMPANY

1501 N. W. 10TH AVENUE

Miami 36, Florida

- 2 -

Oh grant us, Lord, that this may
be the year – when men so eager
now to reach and explore and
colonize other planets, may learn
to live in peaceful brotherhood On
this one.

In our younger days, we probably felt the grass
was always greener beyond the fence, but there should
be many, many better ways to spend these hard-earned
dollars.

Sincerely,

James C McClelland

James C. McClelland
President

JCM/sc

Serving the Medical Profession Since 1926

The White House
Washington

WA018 NL PD

JACKSONVILLE FLO OCT 26   1959 OCT 26 PM 10 31

THE PRESIDENT

    THE WHITE HOUSE

PLEASE SIR INAUGURATE A CRASH SPACE PROGRAM, REGARDLESS OF COST

AND GET AHEAD OF THE RUSSIANS IN THE SPACE RACE STOP WE AMERICANS

DO NOT LIKE BEING A SECOND RATE POWER STOP THE CONSEQUENCE

OF LOSING THIS RACE IS ENSLAVEMENT STOP IT IS NO ONES

RESPONSIBILITY BUT YOURS, AS YOU HAVE BEEN WARNED TIME AND AGAIN OF

THE RUSSIANS PROGRESS

no print in file 11/10/59

THE INTERSTATE SYSTEM

Are we there yet?

If you were born toward the end of the Baby Boom or later, you may consider four-lane interstate highways a birthright. If you were born earlier, you know better.

The interstate highway system as it is known today was an Eisenhower presidential imperative and it contradicts the view of Eisenhower as a hands-off president. The system was a vast social and engineering project that the 34th president believed in and threw his considerable popularity and political capital behind.

Late in World War II, Eisenhower had seen the autobahns of Germany and realized that high-speed, limited-access highways could hasten the movement of large numbers of people, whether troops or residents of cities in times of emergency.

"Germany," he once wrote, "had made me see the wisdom of broader ribbons across the land."

As a veteran of the 62-day military convoy from Washington to San Francisco in 1919, Eisenhower knew that any vast exodus from a large city, even in the 1950s, would have been a disaster. In an emergency evacuation, "our obsolescent highways, too small for the flood of traffic of an entire city's people going one way, would turn into traps of death and destruction."

He had other reasons for proposing new highways. By the mid-1950s, times were good – with peace, prosperity and inflation of about 1 percent. Also, the country was moving around – literally.

"The weight of the nation was shifting," he once wrote. "More people were moving westward."

The car business was booming. In 1955, Detroit automakers sold about 8 million cars, 2 million more than they had the year before. The percentage of families owning cars grew from 60 percent in 1952 to 70 percent in 1955. Every year, he wrote, Americans scrapped more cars than were owned in all of West Germany.

Autos began overwhelming the roads before Eisenhower became president. Except for the Pennsylvania Turnpike and a few other highways in the East, there were almost no four-lane highways connecting urban areas.

That changed after Eisenhower signed the authorization of the Federal-Aid National Highway Act of 1956. In 1990, on the centennial of Eisenhower's birth, President George H.W. Bush named the interstate system the Dwight D. Eisenhower National System of Interstate and Defense Highways.

Its legacy remains vast and complex. Interstate highways expanded the nation's economy, gave generations of Americans a sense of personal possibility unknown to their grandparents, and brought some unintended consequences.

Those included urban sprawl, smog, and – on summer vacations – that familiar question asked of parents by their children, again and again:

Are we there yet?

An outline
of interstate
highway and
other projects.

PLANNING FOR
PUBLIC WORKS

PREPARED UNDER THE DIRECTION OF THE
SPECIAL ASSISTANT TO THE PRESIDENT
FOR PUBLIC WORKS PLANNING

JULY 1957

FOR RELEASE AT 12 NOON (E.S.T.)   February 22, 1955

CAUTION: The following message of the President scheduled for delivery to the Congress today, February 22, 1955, MUST BE HELD IN STRICT CONFIDENCE and no portion, synopsis or intimation may be given out or published UNTIL RELEASE TIME.

The same caution applies to all newspapers, radio and television commentators and news broadcasters, both in the United States and abroad.

PLEASE USE EXTREME CARE TO AVOID PREMATURE PUBLICATION OR ANNOUNCEMENT.

James C. Hagerty
Press Secretary to the President

- -

THE WHITE HOUSE

TO THE CONGRESS OF THE UNITED STATES:

Our unity as a nation is sustained by free communication of thought and by easy transportation of people and goods. The ceaseless flow of information throughout the Republic is matched by individual and commercial movement over a vast system of inter-connected highways crisscrossing the Country and joining at our national borders with friendly neighbors to the north and south.

Together, the uniting forces of our communication and transportation systems are dynamic elements in the very name we bear — United States. Without them, we would be a mere alliance of many separate parts.

The nation's highway system is a gigantic enterprise, one of our largest items of capital investment. Generations have gone into its building. Three million, three hundred and sixty-six thousand miles of road, travelled by 58 million motor vehicles, comprise it. The replacement cost of its drainage and bridge and tunnel works is incalculable. One in every seven Americans gains his livelihood and supports his family out of it. But, in large part, the network is inadequate for the nation's growing needs.

In recognition of this, the Governors in July of last year at my request began a study of both the problem and methods by which the National Government might assist the States in its solution. I appointed in September the President's Advisory Committee on a National Highway Program, headed by Lucius D. Clay, to work with the Governors and to propose a plan of action for submission to the Congress. At the same time, a committee representing departments and agencies of the national Government was organized to conduct studies coordinated with the other two groups.

All three were confronted with inescapable evidence that action, comprehensive and quick and forward-looking, is needed.

First: Each year, more than 36 thousand people are killed and more than a million injured on the highways. To the home where the tragic aftermath of an accident on an unsafe road is a gap in the family circle, the monetary worth of preventing that death cannot be reckoned. But reliable estimates place the measurable economic cost of the highway accident toll to the Nation at more than $4.3 billion a year.

Second: The physical condition of the present road net increases the cost of vehicle operation, according to many estimates, by as much as one cent per mile of vehicle travel. At the present rate of travel, this totals more than $5 billion a year. The cost is not borne by the individual vehicle operator alone. It pyramids into higher expense of doing the nation's business. Increased highway transportation costs, passed on through each step in the distribution of goods, are paid ultimately by the individual consumer.

more

Third: In case of an atomic attack on our key cities, the
road net must permit quick evacuation of target areas, mobil[...]
defense forces and maintenance of every essential economic [...]
But the present system in critical areas would be the breed[...]
deadly congestion within hours of an attack.

Fourth: Our Gross National Product, about $35[...]
1954, is estimated to reach over $500 billion in 1965 wh[...]
population will exceed 180 million and, according to oth[...]
will travel in 81 million vehicles 814 billion vehicle [...]
Unless the present rate of highway improvement and devel[...]
increased, existing traffic jams only faintly foreshadow[...]
years hence.

To correct these deficiencies is an obligation[...]
at every level. The highway system is a public enterpri[...]
owner and operator, the various levels of Government hav[...]
for management that promotes the economy of the nation a[...]
serves the individual user. In the case of the Federal [...]
moreover, expenditures on a highway program are a return to the
highway user of the taxes which he pays in connection with his use of
the highways.

Congress has recognized the national interest in the principal
roads by authorizing two Federal-aid systems, selected cooperatively by
the States, local units and the Bureau of Public Roads.

The Federal-aid primary system as of July 1, 1954, consisted
of 234,407 miles, connecting all the principal cities, county seats,
ports, manufacturing areas and other traffic generating centers.

In 1944 the Congress approved the Federal-aid secondary
system, which on July 1, 1954, totalled 482,972 miles, referred to as
farm-to-market roads -- important feeders linking farms, factories,
distribution outlets and smaller communities with the primary system.

Because some sections of the primary system, from the
viewpoint of national interest are more important than others, the
Congress in 1944 authorized the selection of a special network, not to
exceed 40,000 miles in length, which would connect by routes, as direct
as practicable, the principal metropolitan areas, cities and industrial
centers, serve the national defense, and connect with routes of
continental importance in the Dominion of Canada and the Republic of
Mexico.

This National System of Interstate Highways, although it
embraces only 1.2 percent of total road mileage, joins 42 State
capital cities and 90 percent of all cities over 50,000 population.
It carries more than a seventh of all traffic, a fifth of the rural
traffic, serves 65 percent of the urban and 45 percent of the rural
population. Approximately 37,600 miles have been designated to date.
This system and its mileage are presently included within the
Federal-aid primary system.

In addition to these systems, the Federal Government has the
[...]d in many cases the sole, responsibility for roads that
[...]ide access to Federally owned land -- more than one-fifth
[...]area.

[...]all these, the Interstate System must be given top
[...]onstruction planning. But at the current rate of
[...]the Interstate network would not reach even a reasonable
[...]t and efficiency in half a century. State highway
[...]annot effectively meet the need. Adequate right-of-way
[...]trol of access; grade separation structures; relocation
[...]t of present highways; all these, done on the necessary
[...]an integrated system, exceed their collective capacity.

[...]we have a congested and unsafe and inadequate system, how
[...]mprove it so that ten years from now it will be fitted to
the nation's requirements?

more

VIETNAM

Trying to stop the spread of communism in Asia, the Eisenhower Administration in the 1950s provided military assistance to the pro-western government of South Vietnam. In a 1954 press conference, Eisenhower used the metaphor of a "falling domino," to describe how the fall of one government – such as South Vietnam – to the Communists might cause another and then another to go the same way.

As early as 1955, however, Eisenhower had received a report that the South Vietnamese government of President Ngo Dinh Diem was "no longer supportable." Worse, in one written summary of an April 1955 White House conference with Eisenhower and others, Diem himself was described as "completely intractable" and exhibiting such poor judgment that his government "will inevitably fall."

The United States continued to back Diem and in May 1957 Eisenhower personally welcomed him to the United States. Diem continued to maintain his office, yet U.S. foreign affairs professionals – to judge from documents held by the Eisenhower Library – continued to harbor grave reservations about him.

The Vietnam Communist press lampooned Diem as a tool of capitalists.

UNCLASSIFIED

TOP SECRET

COPY _1_ of 3 copies

ITEM #5

CODE MATERIAL - EIDER

April 22, 1955

MEMORANDUM FOR THE RECORD

Subject: South Vietnam - General Joe Collins' Comments

At a luncheon meeting today at the White House, General Collins
made a report to the President on the current state of affairs in South
Vietnam, in the presence of the following, who attended in addition to the
President: Under Secretary of State Herbert Hoover, Jr.; Under Secretary
of Defense Robert Anderson; and Dillon Anderson.

General Collins said that the state of affairs in Saigon had
reached the point where, in his opinion, the continuation of the present
government under Diem was no longer supportable; that Diem had lost his
Cabinet Ministers one by one and would lose two others as soon as the current phases of their activities were brought to a conclusion; that he had
filled these vacancies by appointing himself to the places formerly occupied
by the Cabinet Ministers, so that he was now his own Minister of Defense,
and I believe Minister likewise of what corresponds to our Interior Department. At any rate - to give an example of his lack of administrative
capability - he is presently signing personally all visas, for entry into
and exit from the country; that he is completely intractable, unwilling
to accept suggestions, and using such poor judgment, as General Collins
sees it, in his efforts to maintain his government, that his government
will inevitably fall.

General Collins mentioned the fact that Diem's two brothers
were installed in the palace and were hovering over the leader, pulling
and tugging all the time.

General Collins went on to describe a number of instances wherein
Diem had been persuaded at only the last minute not to do some utterly
foolish thing, particularly in reference to Collins' and Ely's recommendations to him as to how to handle or deal with the Binh Xuyen Sect, and
this Sect's control of the National Security Police and certain instal-
lations in Saigon. He cited as an example the Diem plan at one time to
attack the heavily armed police headquarters in the heart of Saigon at
1:30 in the afternoon with machine guns and guards, - when the streets were
full of pedestrians and vehicles, and also when a school nearby was letting
out for the day. Many other instances were cited by General Collins, but
the net of it is that he feels now that this fellow is impossible, and the
French share this view, as well. He sees no future for the government so
long as it remains on the course that it is, under the leadership of Diem.

The President asked General Collins if he ascribed the deterioration in the stability of the Diem regime to the French undermining, and
he said, to my surprise, no, he did not altogether. Collins went ahead to

COPY FOR MR. ANDERSON ✓

UNCLASSIFIED

DECLASSIFIED
E.O. 12356, SEC. 3.4 (b)
MR 93-533 #1
BY _____ DATE 6/14/95

TOP SECRET
CODE MATERIAL - EIDER

say he believed that there had been a bonafide effort on the part of the French to bring about some viability of the Diem regime, but that the trouble did not begin recently, when the French concluded they would no longer support Diem. The trouble, said General Collins, went far back of that, and into the very beginning of the efforts of this impossible fellow to form a government. The President said he had understood the facts to be otherwise, and that the undermining of Diem by the French had been a material and substantial contributing cause to the present plight of the government. Collins said he did not wish this repeated outside of the room, but he felt the President had received inadequate and inaccurate intelligence. He expressed the belief that the majority of our intelligence had come from the Palace, and that either the source or the evaluation of the intelligence had not been good.

General Collins told the President of the only plan which he believes is a workable one at this time, — namely, that Quat could be built up and encouraged to take over. He said that Quat could do so, and would do so, only through the intervention of Bao Dai. He said he felt that Quat was the best man on the scene now, and the one most likely to succeed. He said that a Ministry surrounding Quat should include a young man whose name I cannot recall or pronounce, who had at one time been the Minister of Defense. He named several other individuals who in his opinion would rally around Quat and form a government, but that this could only be done under the aegis of Bao Dai. He stated also that Ely concurred in the foregoing views.

Mr. Hoover pointed out that Bao Dai was identified throughout the Far East, and in the American press, as well, as a subsidized French puppet and a symbol of colonialism. He mentioned the possibility that the move suggested by Collins would look like a French move, supported by us. General Collins said he recognized this, but that Bao Dai was a man of more substance than the press gave him credit for being. He spoke of a book he had recently read by a French woman who gave Bao Dai credit for forcing a return of Cochin-China (set aside by the French in 1945 as a colonial plum) into the Associated States as a condition to his return to power.

Under the Collins' plan, he feels that there can be a relinquishment by the Binh Xuyen Sect of the police force, if Quat takes over under Bao Dai. General Collins bases this upon some statements that have been made to some third parties, and apparently the hook-up between Bao Dai and the Binh Xuyen Sect is to be the key to this.

The President said, in substance, that he wanted to know what kind of a plan could be put into effect that would enable us to see whether or not it will be possible to save the area from chaos and communism. General Collins felt that the program he had suggested, though not assured of success or viability, struck him at this time as the best course to be followed in a bad situation. The meeting broke up upon a decision that there will be further study made in the State Department, and that Mansfield would be asked in.

I would say that the session amounted to a mere reporting to the President of the state of affairs, and that no decisions were made.

DILLON ANDERSON
Special Assistant
to the President

Eisenhower with Ngo Dinh Diem in Washington

In 1963, two years after Eisenhower left the presidency, he received a briefing from John McCone, director of the Central Intelligence Agency. McCone was close to Eisenhower, having served as head of the Atomic Energy Commission from 1958 through 1961 in Eisenhower's second term. Their conversation was detailed in a memo declassified in 1996. According to it, the fundamental purpose of McCone's visit was to discuss the volatile political situation in South Vietnam.

By the time of the meeting – eight years after Eisenhower received the unfavorable report on Diem's methods – the South Vietnamese president had grown even more unpopular in his country.

According to the account of the conversation between McCone and Eisenhower, sentiments conflicted within the Kennedy Administration about Diem's future. McCone described two camps. One believed Diem should be removed from power, and the other believed the United States should stick with him.

McCone described W. Averell Harriman, a roving ambassador for Kennedy, as insisting upon Diem's departure. Harriman, McCone was quoted as saying, was trying to "undo everything that President Eisenhower…ever did."

Eisenhower agreed and, according to the memo, described Harriman as "simply stupid."

Less than two months later, Diem was overthrown in a military coup and killed. Scholars of the Vietnam era believe administration officials promised support to South Vietnamese military officers seeking to topple him, although little evidence exist that the Kennedy Administration endorsed his death.

John S. D. Eisenhower   300 CARLISLE STREET, GETTYSBURG, PENNSYLVANIA

September 19, 1963

MEMORANDUM OF CONFERENCE WITH FORMER PRESIDENT EISENHOWER:

OTHERS PRESENT: Honorable John McCone, Director, CIA
                    Mr. John Eisenhower

Before coming to the main topic of conversation General Eisenhower asked
Mr. McCone how the Test Ban Treaty was coming. Mr. McCone said the

*   *   *   *

On General Eisenhower's request Mr. McCone then came to the purpose of his
visit, which turned out to be the situation existing in South Vietnam. He began
by giving the background as he saw it.

measures taken by the Diem regime and prevalent nepotism in his government. For example, Mr. Nhu holds no official position in government but
nevertheless has executed personally the "strategic hamlet" program (which
on the U. S. side was done by the CIA). Mr. McCone represented the strategic hamlet program as being a success, although in the Mekong Delta to the
South only 50% of the villages were at this moment protected.

Up to May 8, Mr. McCone went on, the war was going better, the strategic
hamlet program was underway, and the only cloud on the horizon was the
deterioration on the home front, largely on the part of the intellectual elite.

The first open incident occurred on May 8th and resulted from a Catholic
priest's running up a Catholic flag over a church. The Buddhists had begun
to riot and some shooting resulted. There is no indication that the Buddhists
were Communist-infiltrated, but there are indications of political movements
within that sect. Our government attempted to pressure Diem subtly into in-
stituting less repressive measures, but to no success.

At that time our government had seen no alternative to Diem. The situation
was exacerbated, however, on August 21. On that date some of Diem's
"Special Forces" cut loose and raided some Buddhist pagodas allegedly sus-
pected of harboring subversives. Press criticism of the Diem regime became
very strong. There are two reporters currently in Saigon who are making a
major project of trying to topple the Diem regime. Mr. McCone pointed out
with a straight face that the present Administration listens to the press very
carefully.

There have now developed within the Administration two positions. One, held
by Mr. Harriman and others, insists that Diem must go. Mr. McCone gave
the opinion somewhat sheepishly that Mr. Harriman is largely motivated by
an irrational desire to undo everything that President Eisenhower and Secretary Dulles ever did. General Eisenhower agreed readily and said that while
Harriman is pleasant to himself on the surface, he is undoubtedly attempting
to do this. He described Harriman as simply stupid.

Mr. McCone continued that the other group is led by Secretary McNamara,
who has made a personal war of this Vietnamese engagement. He feels that
the government should go slow in trying to replace Diem, that the war is going well, that we could not rebuild the government under present conditions,
and that any political actions to overthrow the government should certainly
wait until the war is won.

THE BEST DIVERSION

The biggest club in the golf bag is usually the sand wedge. That's the club the president of the United States threw at his doctor in 1959.

In those years, Dwight Eisenhower was the most visible golfer in the country and perhaps the world. He took up the pastime in the 1920s, at his wife's urging, while attending the U.S. Army Command and General Staff College at Fort Leavenworth, Kansas. Eisenhower finished first in his class at the college; perhaps he associated golf with personal achievement.

In April 1948 he wrote longtime friend Everett "Swede" Hazlett about a vacation to Augusta, Georgia, where he had stayed in quarters near the celebrated Augusta National golf course.

"It was the best two weeks I have had in many years," he said.

He would continue to vacation at Augusta throughout his presidency. The Eisenhower Library files contain scorecards of various foursomes there. They testify to the president's occasional birdies.

One rule about golfing with the president: don't discuss business. One day in September 1955, Eisenhower was playing golf in Colorado when he was called away from the 14th green to take a telephone call from John Foster Dulles, his secretary of state.

"The quality of his game collapsed," wrote historian Michael Beschloss.

After 18 holes Eisenhower had dinner, and then went back to the golf course. Twice more, he was interrupted by calls from Dulles. The president was so angry, according to his longtime physician, Howard Snyder, that "the veins stood out on his forehead like whipcords."

The next morning Eisenhower suffered a heart attack.

In 1959, it was Snyder who got the worst of the president's temper. On April 11, Snyder's journals recorded an unremarkable front nine with Eisenhower. But the back nine apparently went poorly from the president's perspective. After a shot out of a sand trap on the 17th hole, Snyder yelled out, "Fine shot."

Big mistake.

Eisenhower yelled, " 'Fine shot, hell, you son of a bitch,' and threw his wedge at me," Snyder wrote. "The staff of the club wrapped itself around my shins and the heavy iron wedge missed me; otherwise, I would have had a fractured leg."

The president apologized with a perfunctory, "Oh, pardon me."

Letters poured into the White House offering advice to Eisenhower on his putting or his swing. Some writers wanted to carry his clubs. He received various clubs and scores of golf balls from individuals or companies.

In the 1960s, after he left the White House, golf was a diversion for a restless former president. In retirement, wrote historian Robert Ferrell, Eisenhower "could not sit still and time seemed to hang on his hands. People noticed the golf games, which were easily reported, and there was talk of much card playing."

For the record: Dwight Eisenhower was the first president or former president to record a hole-in-one. That happened February 6, 1968, on the 13th hole at Seven Lakes Country Club in Palm Springs, California, on a 104-yard par 3.

GENERAL SNYDER'S PROGRESS REPORTS - Saturday,   11 APRIL 1959

0820 - The President went to his office and stayed there until 0852 hours.

0853 - Went out to practice golf and practiced about 40 minutes.

0925 - Teed off for 18 holes of golf with Pete Jones, Sig Larmon, and Albert Bradley

       The President's golf was reasonably good on the first nine, but the worst I have ever seen on the second nine. The President was so mad that on the 17th green when he made a bad explosion shot out of the trap and I yelled, "Fine shot!", he got so mad he yelled, "Fine shot, hell, you son of a bitch," and threw his wedge at me. The staff of the club wrapped itself around my shins and the heavy iron wedge missed me; otherwise, I would have had a fractured leg. He apologized perfunctorily and said, "Oh, pardon me." The game was concluded at 1235 hours.

1240 - Immediately after return from golf and a walk up the steps to the second floor:

          BP: 150/88/88 regular; no reinforced beats

1400 - The President rested until this hour. Had lunch.

1423 - Went to his office and worked there until 1548 hours.

1550 - Returned to the cottage and started a bridge game with Bill Robinson, Sig Larmon, Pete Jones, and Slats Slater. Played until 1830 hours.

1840 - The President met with Allen Dulles and Jerry Greene of the State Department. Mr. Dulles gave a full report on his brother. This meeting lasted until 1925 hours.

1930 - The President, Mamie, Bill Robinson, Mrs. Snyder and I had dinner together.

       After dinner, we sat and watched the Bob Jones pictures of the Masters' Tournament in England and play at St. Andrews in Scotland, where he had been a guest this past summer.

2145 - The President went to bed. Was asleep at 2215 hours.

After a round on the links in the Philippines in 1937.

"Oh, pardon me...." The president issued a mild apology after cursing his physician during a poor round of golf.

211

Using a set of miniature clubs given to him by Dwight and Mamie, grandson David Eisenhower took a swing at the president's Colorado retreat in August 1955.

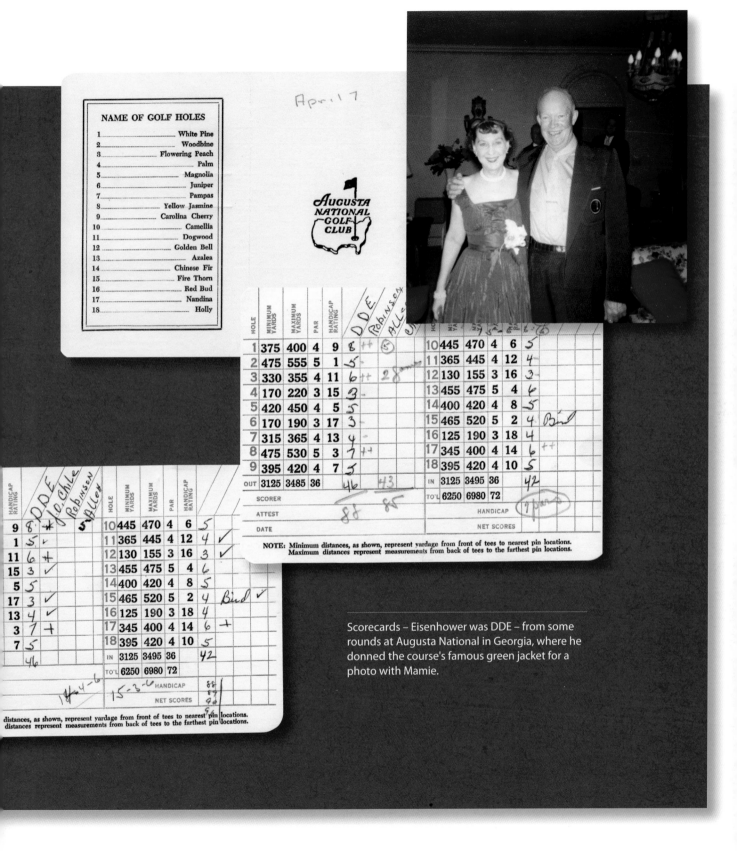

NAME OF GOLF HOLES

1	White Pine
2	Woodbine
3	Flowering Peach
4	Palm
5	Magnolia
6	Juniper
7	Pampas
8	Yellow Jasmine
9	Carolina Cherry
10	Camellia
11	Dogwood
12	Golden Bell
13	Azalea
14	Chinese Fir
15	Fire Thorn
16	Red Bud
17	Nandina
18	Holly

April 7

AUGUSTA NATIONAL GOLF CLUB

HOLE	MINIMUM YARDS	MAXIMUM YARDS	PAR	HANDICAP RATING	DDE
1	375	400	4	9	8
2	475	555	5	1	5
3	330	355	4	11	6
4	170	220	3	15	3
5	420	450	4	5	5
6	170	190	3	17	3
7	315	365	4	13	4
8	475	530	5	3	7
9	395	420	4	7	5
OUT	3125	3485	36		46

HOLE	MINIMUM YARDS	MAXIMUM YARDS	PAR	HANDICAP RATING	DDE
10	445	470	4	6	5
11	365	445	4	12	4
12	130	155	3	16	3
13	455	475	5	4	6
14	400	420	4	8	5
15	465	520	5	2	4	Bird
16	125	190	3	18	4
17	345	400	4	14	6
18	395	420	4	10	5
IN	3125	3495	36		42
TO'L	6250	6980	72		

SCORER 88 85

ATTEST

DATE

HANDICAP

NET SCORES

NOTE: Minimum distances, as shown, represent yardage from front of tees to nearest pin locations. Maximum distances represent measurements from back of tees to the farthest pin locations.

Scorecards – Eisenhower was DDE – from some rounds at Augusta National in Georgia, where he donned the course's famous green jacket for a photo with Mamie.

THE FUR FLIES

On March 25, 1955, a slow news day turned into a long one for Press Secretary James Hagerty. The topic was the president's White House putting green, and the damage done to it by three squirrels. The story had gone on for several days. The press followed it and Democrats in Congress were organizing a save-the-squirrel campaign. That day, Hagerty mentioned to the press that the three squirrels had been removed.

Removed? The press corps sprang to attention. Under questioning, Hagerty revealed that the squirrels had been trapped. Pressed, he said he did not know the details of the trapping, but added that the squirrels had not been harmed in the action.

Questions continued.

Had this action been ordered by the president?

He had noticed the problem, Hagerty said, and had mentioned it.

Two of the squirrels, he said, had been released in the nearby Rock Creek area of the District of Columbia. A third was taken to Virginia.

That brought a new barrage of questions.

Was one squirrel worse than the others?

Didn't the squirrels like each other?

Despite the jesting, one of the last points made by the press corps seemed genuine. After all, they had had to file some kind of story from the otherwise dreary press conference:

"We appreciate this."

MR. HAGERTY'S
NEWS CONFERENCE
MARCH 25, 1955
AT 10:35 AM EST

MR. HAGERTY: Some nominations -- all military. And two bills. And that's all I have this morning, unless you ladies and gentlemen have some questions.

Q. Do you know anything about an emergency board report on a conductors dispute that is supposed to come out here today, they say, at the Labor Department?

MR. HAGERTY: I haven't heard of it. Anybody got anything else?

Q. Is this day as quiet as it looks?

MR. HAGERTY: I hope so -- No -- I have got something. I was reading in the papers lately about a squirrel. And I have read of some comments made.

Actually, the situation is just this: I think it was early last week there was a total number of three squirrels that were harm-lessly trapped, two of them taken to Rock Creek Park and the other to Virginia.

I haven't asked why they were taken to Rock Creek and Virginia, but there have been no other squirrels removed. There has been no other trapping since Thursday of last week, and there will be none in the future. It seems to have cleared up the situation.

Q. That is since Thursday of last week?

MR. HAGERTY: That's right.

Q. Who trapped them?

MR HAGERTY: I don't know. Some of our people.

Q. Who suggested it -- whose idea was it?

MR. HAGERTY: What? I don't know whose idea it was. One of those things that just -- that apparently -- that -- those three were the ones that were causing damage to the green that was put in by the United States Golfing Association for the President of the United States.

Q. Was this a family of squirrels?

MR. HAGERTY: I don't know. I am not a squirrel expert. (laugh)

Q. Why did they take them to more than one place?

MR. HAGERTY: Don't ask me, I don't know.

Q. Was one worse than the other?

Q. Didn't they like each other?

Q. Why was there a decision to trap and remove any squirrels?

According to a transcript of Press Secretary James Hagerty's briefing, reporters showed intense interest in the matter of the squirrels.

MR. HAGERTY: Johnny, you are not a golfer, but ---

Q. I am not a very good one, but ---

MR. HAGERTY: Oh, I'm sorry -- excuse me -- (more laughter) Those were digging up ---

Q. Has that ceased now?

MR. HAGERTY: Yes.

Q. Has the green not suffered any further damage since they have been removed?

MR. HAGERTY: No -- that's right.

Q. The trapping has been discontinued now?

MR. HAGERTY: That's right.

Q. The problem is solved?

MR. HAGERTY: That's right.

Q. You say you don't know who trapped them, was it the Park people or ---

MR. HAGERTY: Our building personnel -- grounds people

Q. Has the President indicated any involvement in the Has he said anything about the green?

MR. HAGERTY: He noticed it, sure -- that's all -- and gentlemen heard him yesterday, he didn't know what they did, he would see if they could -- the President says something and we t it.

Q. If we can clear that up, the President was aware t squirrels were digging in his green?

MR. HAGERTY: Yes.

Q. Then what he meant yesterday when he said he didn' anything about it was he meant the steps which were being taken?

MR. HAGERTY: That's right.

Q. How do you trap a squirrel, with a box -- in a box

MR. HAGERTY: Something like that.

Q. Well, why, after all these days of refusing to discuss this, you suddenly volunteer this information?

MR. HAGERTY: Because I have been getting a lot of questions. As I say, apparently it has all been cleared up now.

Q. Apparently just a couple of maladjusted squirrels.

MR. HAGERTY: No, golfing squirrels.

Q. Democratic squirrels.

MR. HAGERTY: No, golfing -- and there hasn't been anything since last -- I think the last one was last week sometime -- I don't know whether it was Wednesday or Thursday.

Q. Jim, has the White House been getting any mail on this subject?

MR. HAGERTY: A little, I guess -- I haven't seen it. But -- and no other place, on the front lawn or out any place else -- just in that neighborhood.

Q. Did the President want the traps stopped when he read about it, or was it stopped anyway?

MR. HAGERTY: Stopped because the situation cleared up. I might remind you people -- also I should say, if you gentlemen had asked that question Wednesday, that was the answer you would have gotten.

Q. Again, what was the answer today?

MR. HAGERTY: What? I have just told you.

Q. Same thing.

Q. What we asked you Tuesday.

MR. HAGERTY: All right.

Q. Thank you, friend of the furry ones.

Q. We appreciate this.

Q. If Mr. Folliard were here, he would thank you, too.

END

Alsynite Company of America

P.O. BOX 9335 PACIFIC BEACH - 4654 DE SOTO STREET - SAN DIEGO 9. CALIFORNIA
TELEPHONE: HUdson 8-2851 - CABLE ADDRESS "ALSYNITE"

March 30, 1955

Honorable Dwight D. Eisenhower
White House
Washington, D. C.

My dear Mr. President:

Last week, as a fellow Republican and a fellow golfer, I took the liberty of
wiring you with regard to published reports of the annoyance of squirrels on
the White House putting green -- a problem which, I am told, is not uncommon
on putting greens elsewhere in the nation.

It is altogether possible that the persistency of press reports concerning
the "squirrel matter" has caused some embarrassment to you. If such is the
case, I assure you that our company has no intention whatever of contributing
to any further discussion of the subject.

On the other hand, it has also occurred to us that the squirrels, as originally
reported, may present a genuine problem to the White House Staff. On that
assumption, our Research Department has drawn up rather detailed specifications
for a device which, we sincerely feel, may offer a tasteful and thoroughly
practical solution to this problem.

Thus, I am taking still another liberty -- that
drawing of the putting green shield, which I ori
a sample of the material from which it would be
would be equipped with an unobtrusive, low volta
experience indicates, would obstruct squirrels a
entering upon the putting green.

If the shield elicits your interest, we would be
its construction for early delivery to the White
emphasize, if the subject is one which you would
most certainly defer to your desires.

With my very cordial good wishes,

                                        Respectf

                                        ALSYNITE

                                        [signature]

                                        John S.
                                        Presiden

JSB:ec
Encl.

All proposals and quotations are subject to the terms and condition
ALSYNITE COMPANY OF AMERICA FORMERLY ALLIED

April 6, 1955

Dear Mr. Berkson:

Thank you, on behalf of the President,
for your recent letter. Although your
kind offer is being declined, you may
be sure your courtesy in writing as you
did is very much appreciated.

            Sincerely,

            SHERMAN ADAMS

Mr. John S. Berkson
President
Alsynite Company of America
4654 De Soto Street
San Diego 9, California

SQUACKY SQUIRREL CALL CO.

—Made For—
THE HUNTER

—By—
THE HUNTER

"Guaranteed To Call Squirrels"

FLORA - INDIANA

April 7, 1955

The Honorable Dwight D. Eisenhower
President, United States of America
White House
Washington, D. C.

Dear Mr. Eisenhower:

You will find enclosed one of our squirrel calls. Since the Democrats have been giving you so much trouble about the disposal of the squirrels, we hope this little gift will enable you to lessen some of your troubles by being able to assure your friends that you can replenish the supply of squirrels on the White House lawn at your convenience.

Please accept this gift in fun and good faith. Personally, I have been more than satisfied with your handling of the administration.

Wishing you the best of success in the future, I remain

Yours truly,

SQUACKY SQUIRREL CALL CO.

BY: *S. S. Thomson*
S. S. Thomson

sst/pb

Enclosure

An Indiana manufacturer of squirrel calls sent one of his products in jest – in case the president wanted squirrels back.

THE AGE OF TELEVISION

Like all Americans, Dwight Eisenhower adapted quickly to television.

In the late 1940s stations popped up across the country, and networks began feeding them shows – comedy, drama, variety. By 1956 television reached more than 70 percent of American households.

Seeing the impact of the new medium, Eisenhower sought help from actor Robert Montgomery, a veteran of Broadway and later Hollywood. He was familiar to movie fans from films such as "Here Comes Mr. Jordan" and "Lady in the Lake." Politics and policy interested Montgomery; he had been president of the Screen Actors Guild before and after World War II.

In 1952, in Eisenhower's first campaign for president, Montgomery was brought on as a television consultant. Scholars consider that year's Eisenhower campaign innovative in its use of short spot commercials that emphasized the candidate's winning personality.

But by 1954 Eisenhower still wasn't confident about his appearance on television. He wrote Montgomery a memo quoting an unnamed "television expert" who had critiqued an Eisenhower television appearance the evening before.

"He objects to any kind of a striped suit on me – from this angle he thought I looked very badly last evening," Eisenhower wrote. "What do you think about it?"

The same year Eisenhower became the only president to win an Emmy. The award, now on display at the Eisenhower Museum, recognized Eisenhower's "distinguished use and encouragement of the television medium."

Two years later Montgomery was in the White House oval office when Eisenhower addressed the nation on television, announcing he was going to run for a second term.

"A soft-spoken, gentle man," Eisenhower once wrote, "Montgomery always took pains to make certain that the lights were right, that I wore non-reflecting reading glasses, that the furniture and cameras were positioned correctly."

Robert Montgomery suggested ways to face the television and newsreel cameras for Eisenhower's announcement that he would run for a second term. Right: An unnamed "man who came to see me" had some ideas that Eisenhower handed off to Montgomery.

March 16, 1954.

MEMORANDUM FOR

ROBERT MONTGOMERY

A man who came in to see me this morning said that he saw last night's television show while in the company of a "television expert." He had several suggestions.

(a). He suggested a talk some day on physical fitness in America. He urged that Teddy Roosevelt rode this subject hard and always to good effect.

(b). He objects to any kind of a striped suit on me -- from this angle he thought I looked very badly last evening.

(c). He thinks the lens of the television machine is too high when I am sitting at the desk. He pointed out that toward the end of the political campaign of '52, the technicians were setting the lens below normal, for me.

(d). He urges that in some kind of a broadcast I make a direct request on all of the churches of America to offer special prayers on Easter Sunday for (1) peace, and (2) renewal of faith in the destiny of America.

My first reaction to any suggestion of this kind is always to shy off quickly. What do you think about it?

(e). He also believes that we should occasionally refer to some of the past "false prosperity" as prefaced by the "killing of American boys." He said when complaints about prices are met by the bald statement that there is a direct connection between certain prices and killing, that the argument is driven home much better than if stated in milder terms.

I told him I would pass on his comments to you -- that in such matters I have no responsibility whatsoever.

D. D. E.

Academy of Television Arts and Sciences

A NON-PROFIT CORPORATION DEDICATED TO THE ADVANCEMENT OF TELEVISION

August 31st, 1954

Mr. Thomas E. Stephens
Secretary to the President
The White House
Washington, D. C.

Dear Mr. Stephens:

On May 12th last, a letter was sent to you from our Public Relations Director, Mr. Rodney Coulson, explaining that the Executive Board and members of the T.V. Academy wished to express their appreciation to the President for his distinguished television broadcasts.

However, the Board now realizes that the Honorary Life-time Membership in the Academy, which was suggested, is against policy and understandably so.

The Academy has since created a special award, which we would like to present to President Eisenhower.

The inscription reads:

"To Dwight D. Eisenhower, President of the United States, for his effective and dignified use of television.
Presented by the Academy of Television Arts and Sciences, 1954"

It has been suggested that I inquire into the possibility of stopping off in Denver to make the presentation in person, any time during the month of September, subject to the President's convenience. If this could be arranged, it would be greatly appreciated.

I can be reached at the Madison Hotel in New York City.

Respectfully yours,

Don DeFore, President
Academy of Television Arts and Sciences

SUITE 304 · 6525 SUNSET BOULEVARD · HOLLYWOOD 28, CALIFORNIA · HOllywood 3-8942 · HOllywood 3-1161

Giving Ike his Emmy took a while. Academy President Don DeFore broached the topic with the White House in summer 1954. More than a year later, actor George Murphy brought the matter up again; that time, the message got through.

METRO-GOLDWYN-MAYER PICTURES

C U L V E R ~ C I T Y
CALIFORNIA

September 14, 1955

Dear Jim: + P.P.7.50-C

Don DeFore, who is president of the Academy of Television
Arts and Sciences, called me again regarding the following.

You may or may not recall, last year they requested a
message from the President, to be used on their annual TV
Awards Night, which for reasons that you and I understand
was completely impractical.

The Board of Directors of the TV Academy last year voted
the President an honorary "Emmy" (this is the counterpart
to the Motion Picture Academy "Oscar"), and they would
like to present it to him. To be engraved on the miniature
"Emmy" is the following:

   "Academy of Television Arts and Sciences To
   President Dwight D. Eisenhower
   For his distinguished use and encouragement of the
   television medium".

The citation to be engrossed on Parchment reads:

   "Presented to PRESIDENT DWIGHT D. EISENHOWER as
   a special award in recognition of the professional
   manner in which he has made use of the television
   camera and microphone for his personal messages to
   the people of America; and also for his advocacy
   and practice of the use of television by the Cabinet
   of the United States and other branches of the
   Government, thus encouraging a wider use of the
   medium by men and women important in public life."

It occurred to me that some time when DeFore is in the East
he might be permitted to stop at the White House and present
the "Emmy" to the Boss, with a cameraman present. It is my
feeling that this could not do any harm, and might very well
do some good. Also, Don is a nice guy who would not be a
nuisance or take up any of the Boss' time.

If you feel this can be handled, drop me a line and I'll
set it up.

                    Sincerely,

                    Murph
                    George Murphy

Mr. James Hagerty
White House - Denver, Col.
NO AGREEMENT OR ORDER WILL BE BINDING ON THIS CORPORATION UNLESS IN WRITING AND SIGNED BY AN OFFICER

SPY PLANE SHOT DOWN

In November 1954, President Eisenhower authorized the building of 30 high-flying planes to spy on the Soviet Union. He had worried about political difficulties if the program was revealed to the world, but Secretary of State John Foster Dulles reassured him, saying, "We could live through them." The aircraft, called the U-2, began flying in 1956.

"It was agreed," according to a White House memo in 1959, "that in case of protest, we would defend ourselves with an absolute disavowal and denial on the matter."

Flights were suspended later that year, and on April 25, 1960, the president authorized "one additional operation."

It ended in disaster. On May 1, word reached Eisenhower at Camp David that the U-2 had been shot down. The pilot, Francis Gary Powers, bailed out and was captured by the Soviets. At first, the United States claimed the mission was only to study weather patterns. Within days, the truth came out.

Revelation of the failed mission and the worldwide uproar that followed proved awkward for Eisenhower. According to biographer Stephen Ambrose, he briefly told secretary Ann Whitman that he was ready to resign during the uproar.

Meanwhile, a summit of the superpowers later in May, where Eisenhower had hoped to push for a ban on nuclear tests, collapsed after Soviet Premier Nikita Khrushchev berated the United States for the spy plane program.

The U-2 affair appeared to take the wind out of Eisenhower's sails during the last months of his presidency. Historian Michael Beschloss cites presidential physician Howard Snyder as saying the president "lost his sparkle."

But Eisenhower did not apologize. As an open society, he contended, the United States was at a disadvantage trusting a secretive superpower with demonstrated ambitions of expansion. It had to have a spying program.

As Eisenhower wrote in his 1963 memoir, *Waging Peace*, "I felt anything but apologetic."

Facing page: Details of Eisenhower's approval of plans to build a new spy aircraft.

November 24, 1954

MEMORANDUM OF CONFERENCE WITH THE PRESIDENT
0810   24 November 1954

Others present: Secretary of State
                       (for part of meeting)
                    Secretary of Defense
                    Mr. Allen Dulles
                    Secretary of Air Force
                    General Twining
                    Lt. General Cabell
                    Lt. General Putt
                    Colonel Goodpaster

Authorization was sought from the President to go ahead on a program to produce thirty special high performance aircraft at a cost of about $35 million.   The President approved this action.   Mr. Allen Dulles indicated that his organization could not finance this whole sum without drawing attention to it, and it was agreed that Defense would seek to carry a substantial part of the financing.

The Secretary of Defense sought the President's agreement to taking one last look at the type of operations planned when the aircraft are available.   The President indicated agreement.

To a question by the President, the Secretary of State indicated that difficulties might arise out of these operations, but that "we could live through them."

In summary, the President directed those present to go ahead and get the equipment, but before initiating operations to come in for one last look at the plans.

A. J. Goodpaster

July 8, 1959

MEMORANDUM OF CONFERENCE WITH THE PRESIDENT
July 8, 1959

Others present: Secretary Herter
                    Mr. Allen Dulles
                    Mr. Bissell
                    General Goodpaster

The President said he had asked for the meeting because he wanted to hear Mr. Herter's views about a proposal for a reconnaissance flight. He expressed his own concern over the possibility of getting involved in something costly and harmful.

Mr. Herter said that the intelligence objective in his view outweighs the danger of getting trapped. He noted that a single operation was being proposed. He recognized that there is always the chance of loss of the plane, but our experience has been very good. He had been much interested in the idea of a flight straight through, but understood that this was not practicable. Mr. Dulles confirmed this, commenting that the proposed flight will enter through one country and leave through another.

It was agreed that, in case of protest, we would defend ourselves with an absolute disavowal and denial on the matter.

Mr. Bissell said that the Soviets have a fighter which could probably zoom to the altitude of this plane.

The President then said that Khrushchev seems almost to be looking for excuses to be belligerent. By doing nothing he can put us in a terrible hole in Berlin. Holding the cards he does, he could very readily say that such an event as this marks the end of serious negotiations. There remains in the President's mind the question whether we are getting to the point where we must decide if we are trying to prepare to fight a war, or to prevent one.

> After all the discussion, the President indicated that in view of the unanimous recommendation of the officials having the operating responsibility, he would assent to the operation being conducted.

A. J. Goodpaster
Brigadier General, USA

After hearing arguments from intelligence officials about the need for a spy plane flight over the Soviet Union, Eisenhower gave the OK. The planned route called for the U-2 to fly into the Soviet Union from a base in Pakistan and then return to another base. A Soviet map, far right, marked where the plane was shot down.

April 25, 1960

MEMORANDUM FOR RECORD:

After checking with the President, I informed M[r.]

Bissell that one additional operation may be unde[r]

taken, provided it is carried out prior to May 1.

No operation is to be carried out after May 1.

A. J. Goodpas[ter]

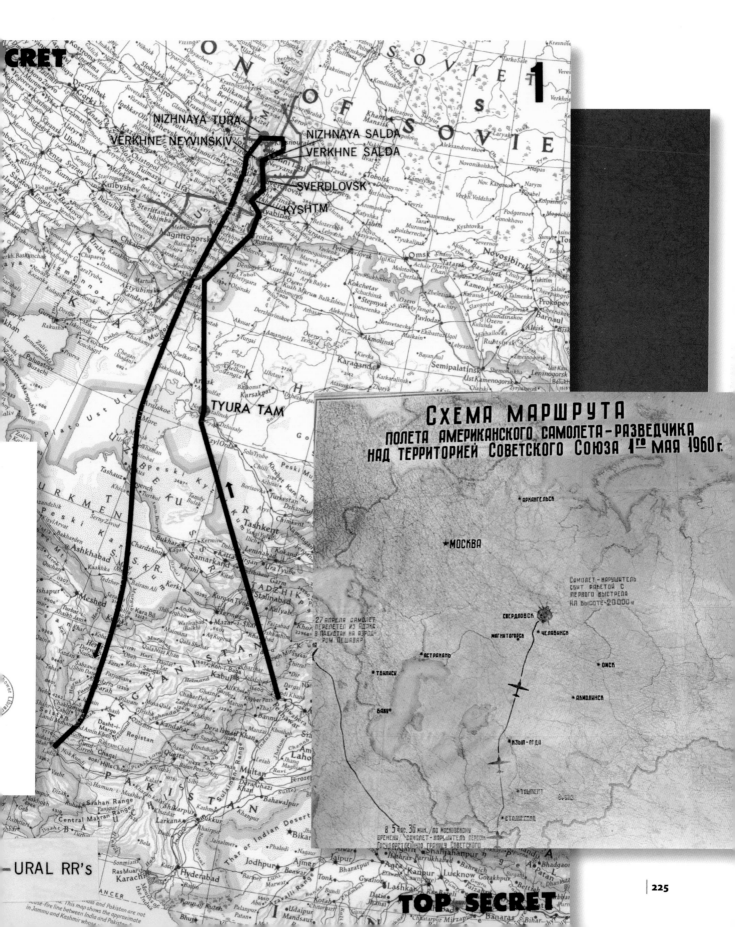

1

NIZHNAYA TURA
VERKHNE NEYVINSKIV

NIZHNAYA SALDA
VERKHNE SALDA

SVERDLOVSK

KYSHTM

TYURA TAM

СХЕМА МАРШРУТА
ПОЛЕТА АМЕРИКАНСКОГО САМОЛЕТА-РАЗВЕДЧИКА
НАД ТЕРРИТОРИЕЙ СОВЕТСКОГО СОЮЗА 1го МАЯ 1960 г.

* АРХАНГЕЛЬСК

★ МОСКВА

27 АПРЕЛЯ САМОЛЕТ
ПЕРЕЛЕТЕЛ ИЗ АДАНА
В ПАКИСТАН НА АЭРО-
ДРОМ ПЕШАВАР

САМОЛЕТ-НАРУШИТЕЛЬ
СБИТ РАКЕТОЙ С
ПЕРВОГО ВЫСТРЕЛА
НА ВЫСОТЕ 20000 м

СВЕРДЛОВСК

МАГНИТОГОРСК   ЧЕЛЯБИНСК

* АСТРАХАНЬ

* ОМСК

* ТБИЛИСИ

* АКМОЛИНСК

БАКУ*

* КЗЫЛ-ОРДА

* ТАШКЕНТ

8 5 час. 36 мин. /ПО МОСКОВСКОМУ
ВРЕМЕНИ/ САМОЛЕТ-НАРУШИТЕЛЬ ПЕРЕСЕК
ГОСУДАРСТВЕННУЮ ГРАНИЦУ СОВЕТСКОГО

* СТАЛИНАБАД

— URAL RR's

TOP SECRET

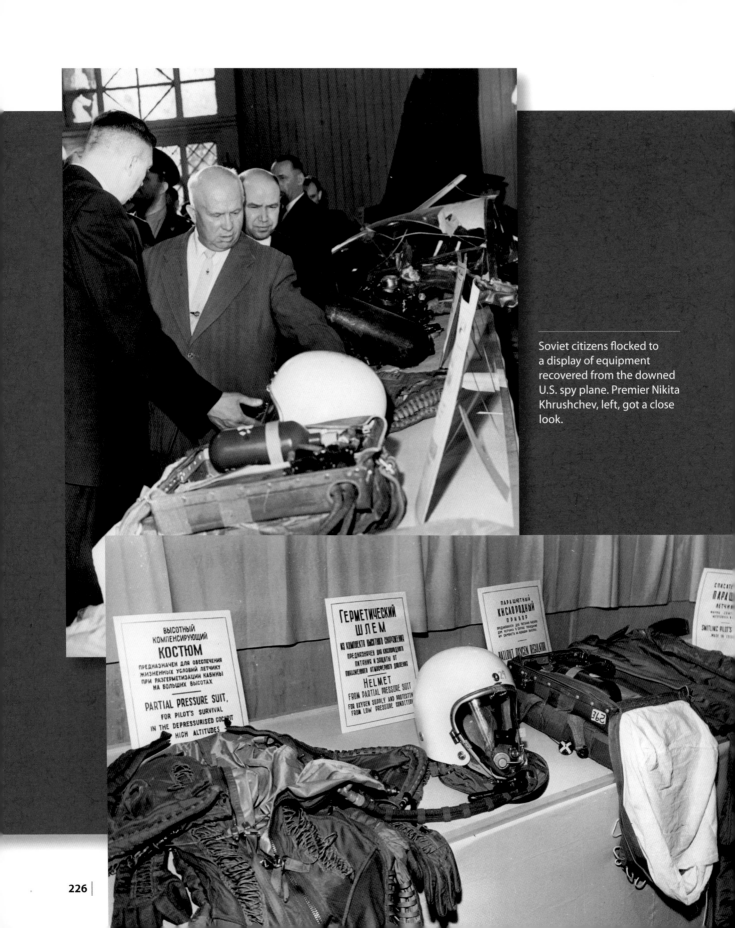

Soviet citizens flocked to a display of equipment recovered from the downed U.S. spy plane. Premier Nikita Khrushchev, left, got a close look.

ВЫСОТНЫЙ
КОМПЕНСИРУЮЩИЙ
КОСТЮМ
ПРЕДНАЗНАЧЕН ДЛЯ ОБЕСПЕЧЕНИЯ
ЖИЗНЕННЫХ УСЛОВИЙ ЛЕТЧИКУ
ПРИ РАЗГЕРМЕТИЗАЦИИ КАБИНЫ
НА БОЛЬШИХ ВЫСОТАХ

PARTIAL PRESSURE SUIT,
FOR PILOT'S SURVIVAL
IN THE DEPRESSURISED COCKPIT
HIGH ALTITUDES

ГЕРМЕТИЧЕСКИЙ
ШЛЕМ
ИЗ КОМПЛЕКТА ВЫСОТНОГО СНАРЯЖЕНИЯ
ПРЕДНАЗНАЧЕН ДЛЯ КИСЛОРОДНОГО
ПИТАНИЯ И ЗАЩИТЫ ОТ
ПОНИЖЕННОГО АТМОСФЕРНОГО ДАВЛЕНИЯ

HELMET
FROM PARTIAL PRESSURE SUIT
FOR OXYGEN SUPPLY AND PROTECTION
FROM LOW PRESSURE CONDITIONS

ПАРАШЮТНЫЙ
КИСЛОРОДНЫЙ
ПРИБОР
ПРЕДНАЗНАЧЕН ДЛЯ ПИТАНИЯ КИСЛО-
РОДОМ ЛЕТЧИКА В СЛУЧАЕ ПОКИДАНИЯ
ИМ САМОЛЕТА НА БОЛЬШОЙ ВЫСОТЕ

BAILOUT OXYGEN RESPIRATOR

СПАСАТЕ
ПАРАШ
ЛЕТЧИ

SMITLING PILOT'S
MADE IN 195

WAR IS NOT AN OPTION

CHECKED BY KARDEX

In the 1960s the phrase "mutual assured destruction" described a possible solution to the danger of nuclear war: If a superpower that began a nuclear conflict could not hope to survive it – if both sides were assured of destruction – then no superpower would want to start a war.

In 1956 President Dwight Eisenhower circled the same idea. In a letter to New York publisher Richard L. Simon, the president suggested that technology perhaps had made large-scale warfare obsolete.

Americans, Eisenhower wrote Simon, "are rapidly getting to the point that no war can be won." Victory in such an era, he added, suggested "destruction of the enemy and suicide for ourselves…an outlook that neither side can ignore.…" It might be time, then, to resolve issues through negotiation.

Possibly, Eisenhower was trying to transcend nuclear deadlock rather than live with the apparent "peace" of a standoff.

April 4, 1956

Personal and Confidential

Dear Dick:

Thank you for your letter, which brings up subjects too vast to be discussed adequately in a letter.

Suffice it to say here that I doubt that any columnist -- and here I depend upon heresay as I have no time to read them -- is concerning himself with what is the true security problem of the day.   That problem is not merely man against man or nation against nation.   It is man against war.

xOF135

I have spent my life in the study of military strength as a deterrent to war, and in the character of military armaments necessary to win a war.   The study of the first of these questions is still profitable, but we are rapidly getting to the point that no war can be won.   War implies a contest; when you get to the point that contest is no longer involved and the outlook comes close to destruction of the enemy and suicide for ourselves -- an outlook that neither side can ignore -- then arguments as to the exact amount of available strength as compared to somebody else's are no longer the vital issues.

xPPFI-

xOF154

xOF154

When we get to the point, as we one day will, that both sides know that in any outbreak of general hostilities, regardless of the element of surprise, destruction will be both reciprocal and complete, possibly we will have sense enough to meet at the conference table with the understanding that the era of armaments has ended and the human race must conform its actions to this truth or die.

xOF13

Personal and Confidential

National Defense

The fullness of this potentiality has not yet been attained, and I do not, by any means, decry the need for strength. That strength must be spiritual, economic and military. All three are important and they are not mutually exclusive. They are all part of and the product of the American genius, the American will.

But already we have come to the point where safety cannot be assumed by arms alone. But I repeat that their usefulness becomes concentrated more and more in their characteristics as deterrents than in instruments with which to obtain victory over opponents as in 1945. In this regard, today we are further separated from the end of World War II than the beginning of the century was separated from the beginning of the sixteenth century.

Naturally I am not taking the time here to discuss the usefulness of available military strength in putting out "prairie fires" -- spots where American interests are seriously jeopardized by unjustified outbreaks of minor wars. I have contented myself with a few observations on the implications of a major arms race.

Finally, I do not believe that I shall ever have to defend myself against the charge that I am indifferent to the fate of my countrymen, and I assure you that there are experts, technicians, philosophers and advisers here, who give far more intelligent attention to these matters than do the Alsops.

With warm regard,

Sincerely,

Mr. Richard L. Simon
Simon and Schuster, Inc.
630 Fifth Avenue
New York 20, New York

The Alsops referred to dismissively in the last paragraph of Eisenhower's letter were syndicated newspaper columnists.

The standoff had been nerve-racking. In 1950 President Harry Truman announced his decision to develop the hydrogen bomb. In 1953 the Soviets announced that they, too, possessed such technology. The next year, federal authorities conducted the "Bravo" hydrogen bomb test at Bikini Atoll in the Pacific. In June 1955 Eisenhower evacuated the White House in a high-profile air raid drill.

Simon had written Eisenhower to promote development of the nation's long-range air power, missiles and air defense. Simon compared those efforts to the program for constructing fighter planes that had helped England endure in the early years of World War II.

Simon checked to be sure Eisenhower's reply was confidential. Ann Whitman, presidential secretary, confirmed that, adding that Simon could show the letter to his wife and a few friends, but that it could not be copied or leaked to the press.

Some presidents forever will own certain phrases.

For Dwight Eisenhower, the phrase is "military-industrial complex."

The term originated in his farewell address to the country, made on national television January 17, 1961.

"In the councils of government," Eisenhower said, "we must guard against the acquisition of unwarranted influence, whether sought or unsought, by the military-industrial complex. The potential for the disastrous rise of misplaced power exists and will persist."

Ever since, the speech has been cited as prescient and made all the more grave because it was delivered by a man who also was his generation's most accomplished soldier.

The phrase evidently originated with Ralph Williams, who served as assistant Naval aide in the White House. Williams, with principal speechwriter Malcolm Moos, contributed to the farewell address. In a 1988 Eisenhower Library oral history, Williams specifically recalled changing one phrase from "war-based industrial complex" to "military industrial complex."

Eisenhower was a hands-on participant in the writing of his speeches, Williams recalled. Important ones went through as many as 12 to 15 drafts. The Eisenhower Library, for instance, has seven drafts of the farewell address generated from January 6 to January 16 alone.

Williams' phrase apparently resonated with Eisenhower, who had long worked within, keenly understood and often expressed reservations about what had come to be called the national-security state. Eisenhower did little editing of that section, probably the best evidence that Williams had turned a phrase that captured the president's concern.

A reading copy of the address, with many phrases underlined, suggests Eisenhower's active participation. No matter how much he or Moos may have contributed to the address, Williams said in 1988, its ultimate author was Eisenhower.

"He said it and he understood it and he meant it," Williams said, "and he is the author and nobody else has any claim to the authorship of that speech because, as you can see, he was not a man to let anybody put words in his mouth.

"If he said those words, he meant them."

Facing page: The idea of addressing the "merchants of death" cropped up in planning for Eisenhower's last State of the Union address. It came to fruition in his televised farewell address to Americans.

31 October 1960

MEMORANDUM FOR FILE

Subject: State of the Union 1961

Conversation with Dr. Moos this morning produced following
preliminary guide lines:

1. The problem of militarism -- for the first time in its history, the United States has a permanent war-based industry --
aircraft, 90% -- missiles, 100%, etc. Not only that but flag
and general officers retiring at an early age take positions in
war based industrial complex shaping its decisions and guiding
the direction of its tremendous thrust. This creates a danger
that what the Communists have always said about us may become true. We must be very careful to insure that the "merchants of death do not come to dictate national policy".

2. Over the past year there has been a world wide tendency
for orderly societies to break down into mob ridden anarchies,
e.g. student riots, the Congo, Cuba, etc. In our own country
we see instances where political decisions are first on the
barricades instead of normal governmental processes. It is
easy to wave banners to riot, to protest, but the difficult thing
is to work a constructive change so that society is strengthened
rather than weakened and divided.

3. Analyze previous major addresses of DDE. (Get Eisenhower's
~~speaks~~ from Military Aide's office)

Ralph E. Williams

VESTED IN MY SUCCESSOR.

THIS EVENING I COME TO
YOU WITH A MESSAGE OF
LEAVE TAKING AND
FAREWELL, AND TO SHARE
A FEW FINAL THOUGHTS

Scroll containing the text of
Eisenhower's farewell address, above,
and the edited reading copy, right.

First, I must express my gratitude to
the radio and television networks of the
nation for the opportunities they have given
me, over the years, to bring special messages
to our people. My special thanks go to them
for the opportunity of addressing you this evening

MY FELLOW AMERICANS

THREE DAYS from now,
after half a century in the service
of our country, I shall lay down
the responsibilities of office as,
in traditional and solemn ceremony,
the authority of the Presidency
is vested in my successor.

THIS EVENING I come to you
with a message of leave-taking
and farewell, and to share
a few final thoughts with you,
my countrymen.

13

AMERICAN MAKERS of plowshares could, with time and as required, make swords as well.

But now we can no longer risk emergency improvisation of national defense; we have been compelled to create a permanent armaments industry of vast proportions.

Added to this, three and a half million men and women are directly engaged in the defense establishment.

WE ANNUALLY spend on military security more than the net income of all United States Corporations.

14

THIS CONJUNCTION of an immense military establishment and a large arms industry is new in the American experience.

The total influence -- economic, political, even spiritual -- is felt in every city, every State house, every office of the Federal government.

We recognize the imperative need for this development.

Yet we must not fail to comprehend its grave implications.

Our toil, resources and livelihood are all involved; so is the very structure of our society.

IN THE COUNCILS of government, we must guard against the acquisition of unwarranted influence, whether sought or unsought, by the military-industrial complex.

The potential for the disastrous rise of misplaced power exists and will persist.

WE MUST NEVER let the weight of this combination endanger our liberties or democratic processes.

We should take nothing for granted.

SLOW BOILS, HIGH BLOOD PRESSURE

Dwight Eisenhower's familiar, dazzling smile had a dark counterpart. That was the grim, taut mask his face became when he grew angry and struggled to conceal it.

Many of Eisenhower's biographers speak of how Eisenhower tried with little success to cover up irritation. Michael Korda describes the slow burn Eisenhower endured in the 1930s when his boss, Douglas MacArthur, ordered him to perform a menial task. During Eisenhower's second term, according to Stephen Ambrose, reporters grew bold to ask him about his moods in press conferences.

Mamie Eisenhower confessed to friends during the second term that she became alarmed when anger caused veins in her husband's forehead to grow prominent.

First-hand, expert testimony of the toll that Eisenhower's controlled anger took can be found in the logs of Howard Snyder, Eisenhower's physician. Snyder – himself the object of Eisenhower's wrath in 1959 when he was struck by a golf club thrown by an angry president – watched as Eisenhower's mood soured during an October 1960 campaign stop in Detroit. Someone had handed the president a brochure that characterized a vote for Republicans as a "vote for bigotry."

As Snyder described it, Eisenhower's "lips were so tight that he could hardly smile." Snyder took Eisenhower's blood pressure, revealing an arrhythmia that Snyder treated with medication.

At the time, some had wondered why Eisenhower did so little campaigning for his vice president, Richard Nixon, when he ran for president. Whatever Eisenhower's ultimate opinion about Nixon, he had to honor his doctor's orders to rest - and the campaign trail would have allowed him little of that.

1445 - I took his blood pressure. He had about 12 extra systoles per minute at the wrist on counting his pulse, and in the blood pressure cuff it was all over the map. I could hear a number of beats at 150. The same was true on the diastolic side, the extra systoles coming through down to 74, but the major number of beats fading out about 86 to 84. His pulse rate was 90, counting the skips.

He had had a couple of drinks before lunch. Earlier he had been very upset because of a leaflet that UAW-CIO-AFL had had published and were distributing by the millions, stating, "A vote for Kennedy is a vote for liberty; a vote for Nixon is a vote for bigotry." When he received the Key to the City of Detroit and made a brief response, his lips were so tight that he could hardly smile. He stumbled for words and did not express himself well, but the idea he tried to get across was that everyone in America should go to the poles and vote, but they should vote according to their consciences and not because of the influence of written or other propagandist statements which would divide America and which were entirely destructive of the ideals of American ethical standards. This was the cause, I am sure, of the President's bizarre cardiac action.

I gave him one tablet of QUINIDINE SULFATE, 0.2 gm. He was to rest until 1645 hours.

1600 - Moaney called me. When I came in, the President said he thought his pulse was more irregular than it had been when I took it earlier. This, in fact, was true. There were approximately 20 pre-systoles in every minute of pulse count. The same erratic registration of systoles was noted in the cuff of the sphygmomanometer, the systolic pressure being audible on irregular beats at 160. There was no point between the highest systolic and the lowest diastolic impulse at which the heart beat came through regularly. I could hear the extra systoles on the diastolic side down to 74, but most of the beats faded out at 86 to 84. The pulse, including the skips, was approximately 96 to 100 beats per minute. This despite the fact that the President said he had slept soundly during most of the period between 1445 and 1600 hours.

He was still resting in bed, but had sent for his speech and began to work on it immediately.

1700 - I gave him a second tablet of QUINIDINE SULFATE, 0.2 gm.

1715 - While the President was still lying down, having concluded working on his speech and picked up a western novel, the arrhythmia greatly disappeared. There were approximately 8 extra systoles per minute. The same held true with his blood pressure, which registered 146/86 with only occasional systoles coming through.

(more)

Eisenhower dabbled with painting as a hobby in the 1940s and continued through his White House years. He pursued it in retirement at his farm near Gettysburg. His easel and case of oil paints are at the Eisenhower Library and Museum, along with several paintings.

AN EX-PRESIDENT

After they left the White House in 1961, Dwight and Mamie Eisenhower moved to a 190-acre farm near the Gettysburg Civil War battlefield in southern Pennsylvania. There, they became perhaps the country's most public private citizens.

Freed from the protocols of power, the former president obtained a license and started driving himself for the first time since 1935. Meanwhile, some Americans apparently felt a powerful proprietary interest in the Eisenhowers. According to a biography of her grandmother by Susan Eisenhower, tourists visiting the Gettysburg battlefield sometimes made their way to the Eisenhower home and knocked on the door.

For about four years after the Eisenhowers left the White House, there were no Secret Service personnel about. In the wake of the assassination of President John Kennedy, a law signed by President Lyndon Johnson in 1965 gave former presidents Secret Service protection.

Like many retired Americans, the retired president played golf. Sometimes he left Gettysburg to visit Augusta National golf club in Georgia. In addition, he kept cattle and horses, and also painted. In a sun room of their new home, Dwight and Mamie played board games.

He was, nevertheless, a former president and so received visits from Kennedy Administration figures who briefed him on issues. He remained interested in Republican politics, and offered advice for Ronald Reagan, elected governor of California in 1966.

Mamie, meanwhile, volunteered for the American Heart Association. She accepted Jacqueline Kennedy's invitation to be a fund-raising co-chair for the National Cultural Center in Washington, which was authorized by President Eisenhower in 1958. After Kennedy's assassination, the building was renamed the Kennedy Center for the Performing Arts.

As for the cultural upheavals of the 1960s, the Eisenhowers' regard for them is easy to imagine. According to granddaughter Susan, "many of the values that my grandparents had spent their lives advancing – Duty, Honor, Country – were increasingly ridiculed as outdated or irrelevant."

REMEMBERING D-DAY

In preparation for the 20th anniversary of the D-Day landings in World War II, CBS arranged for Eisenhower to return to his old headquarters in Great Britain and to the beaches and military cemeteries of France. In August 1963, he filmed a television special with Walter Cronkite.

Eisenhower's return, Cronkite recalled on National Public Radio in 2004, "was to be a special valedictory." He remembered how Eisenhower characterized the visit – "an adventure in nostalgia." Crossing the Atlantic by ocean liner, they went first to Portsmouth, the Allied forward headquarters where the decision to go was made on June 5, 1944. Then they crossed the English Channel to Omaha Beach in Normandy on the northwest coast of France.

They went inside an old German bunker to survey the scene, Cronkite remembered. A few rusted obstacles were the only reminders on a pleasant day in 1963. Sailboats plied the waters along the coast.

"The tranquility of the scene was hard to reconcile with the images...of D-Day," Cronkite said.

Years later, Cronkite recalled that the visit marked Eisenhower's first extended walk on those beaches since the invasion itself.

In the American military cemetery overlooking Omaha

Weapons and other equipment found on the beaches of Normandy decades after D-Day. They are on display at the Eisenhower Library and Museum.

Before Eisenhower departed for Europe with the CBS crews, he received this letter from the mother of a GI who died in the invasion. She asked him to say a silent prayer at the cemetery.

FKK   July 17-63

Dear Mr. President (you will always be this to us)

    When you make your mission to Normandy — St. Laurent-France is the cemetery — when you pass a grave Pfc. Herbert Kaufman - 15382485 Plot B- Row 10 - Grave 188- when you go by, please say a silent prayer for our darling Boy —

    wish we could be there, but this will help- Thanks.

                    Mrs. A. H. Kaufman his Mother

MRS. A. H. KAUFMAN
532 South Sixth
Terre Haute, Indiana

Gettysburg, Pennsylvania
July 26, 1963

Dear Mrs. Kaufman:

General Eisenhower asked me to respond to your letter
of July 17th.

At this moment it is not certain whether the General will
actually visit the cemetary at St. Laurent, France but
should this occur, his secretary or staff assistant will
have knowledge of your request.

Thank you for writing as you did.

With General Eisenhower's best wishes,

Sincerely,

ROBERT L. SCHULZ
Brig. Gen., U.S.A. (Ret
Executive Assistant

Mrs. A. H. Kaufman
532 South Sixth
Terre Haute, Indiana

bcc: Rusty Brown *along with a copy of incom*

Gettysburg, Pennsylvania
August 16, 1963

PERSONAL

Dear Mrs. Kaufman:

General Eisenhower has asked me to forward to you
the enclosed photographs which were taken at your
son's grave in St. Laurent, France. It was at Mrs.
Eisenhower's suggestion that the bouquet was placed
on the grave.

I feel certain that you will be interested in the television
program to commemorate D-Day's twentieth anniversary
in June 1964. This program will have scenes taken at
the cemetary just after these photographs were taken.

General and Mrs. Eisenhower have asked me to convey
to you their kind regard,

Sincerely,

Lillian H. Brown

In an early response to the request by
Mrs. A. H. Kaufman that Eisenhower
say a silent prayer at the grave of
her son, an aide stated that plans
were uncertain. As it turned out,
Eisenhower did visit the grave and
Mamie Eisenhower saw to it that
flowers were placed there.

aug 26 - 63

FKK

Dear Miss Brown:

The Photograph of our Sons
grave. with Pres. Eisenhower by it.
Came this morning - we will always
Treasure it.

Please convey our appreciation
to the Pres & his lovely wife for
being so thoughtful. the flowers
are beautiful - I simply cant find
the right words to thank them
both enough.

Sincerely
Mrs. & Mr. A. H. Kaufman

Beach, Eisenhower reflected on the "inequity of sacrifice." He recalled that his son, John Eisenhower, graduated from West Point that day, fortunate to be far from the front and to live a full life since.

Referring to the tombstones, Eisenhower continued:

"These young boys...were cut off in their prime. They never knew the great experiences of going through life...but these people gave us a chance....

"Every day I think about that day, I say once more: We must find some way to gain an eternal peace for this world."

In January 1965, Winston Churchill died and Dwight Eisenhower sat down to fashion a eulogy for his brother-in-arms from World War II. In fact, Eisenhower and Churchill had worked together officially twice, first while making plans to defeat the Nazis, and again in the mid-1950s, when Churchill's second stint as prime minister overlapped part of Eisenhower's first term in the White House.

The two had had their disagreements. In the 1950s, Churchill apparently was disappointed that Eisenhower hadn't responded to his urging more vigorous diplomatic engagement with the Soviet Union.

Whatever their differences, they did not prevent Eisenhower from writing a heartfelt tribute after the Briton's death.

Drafts of his eulogy also show how Eisenhower's message evolved. A handwritten draft ended, "Here was a man!" A later typed copy, still tweaked by Eisenhower, finishes with phrase used by Shakespeare in Hamlet: "He was a man."

Tribute To Sir Winston Churchill
by Dwight D Eisenhower

all other free men,   personal

As I, like the rest of the world, pause to pay a last tribute

to the giant who now passes from among us, I have no charter to speak

for my countrymen -- only for myself.

                                     two decades   time
But, if in memory we journey back a score of years to the day

when America and Britain stood shoulder to shoulder in global conflict

against tyranny, then I can presume to act as spokesman for the millions

                              with
of Americans who served/me and with their British comrades during three

years of war in this region of the earth.

        To those men Winston Churchill was Britain -- he was the embodiment

of British defiance to threat, her courage in adversity, her calmness in

danger, her modesty in success. Among them his name was spoken with

                                           knew
respect, admiration and affection. They felt he was a staunch ally and an
felt the inspiration of his leadership. They
inspirational leader. Truly a fighter in their ranks.

                                          with   many months
        I was one of those Americans. Like them I was for three years
        Allied   jointly
subject to the military authority he exercised jointly with the President of

                                            days
the United States. During those dramatic months I was privileged to meet,

to talk, to plan and to work with him. Out of that association a friendship

                                        inescapable in the atmosphere
was forged; it stood the trails and tests imposed by the problems of war.
        later and more   imposed by   both were
It flowered in the subtlest tests of international politics when each of us in

incontestable refrain: here was a man.

Winston Churchill was a man,

HE

(handwritten notes, left page):

Winston Churchill, soldier-statesman,
dynamic leader, steady citizen.

describe his accomplishments
and extol his virtues
among all the
soldier statesman,
steady citizen that he was

Here was a man!

At this moment, as our heart

A GIFT

October 1, 1963

Dear Susan:

From Miss Brown I learned that you could give a good home to a horse that I should like to give you. Her name is Quinine and she is a cross between a registered Arabian and a registered Quarter Horse. I shall leave instructions at my Farm for the horse to be available at any time you might want to have her picked up and this letter will be your evidence of ownership.

I want nothing but a good home for her and this I am sure you will give.

With best wishes,

Sincerely,

Miss Susan Markley
39 East Broadway
Gettysburg, Pennsylvania

Dwight Eisenhower was capable of the remarkable magnanimous gesture.

In October 1963 he presented a horse to Susan Markley, the daughter of a secretary in Eisenhower's Gettysburg offices who had died suddenly the previous summer.

"I want nothing but a good home for her and this I am sure you will give," Eisenhower wrote Markley, concerning the horse.

"You have made me more than happy," she wrote back later that month.

October 29

Dear General Eisenhower,
It is extremely
difficult to express my
feelings toward your
great gift. Ever since
I can remember my
dream has been to own
a house. I have worked
hard for many people,
including Mrs. Good,
trying to earn enough
money to someday buy
my own house. When
I heard about my offer
to receive a house whose
name is Quinne at
the Eisenhower farm
I was speechless for
quite a period. I have
the house and is the most beautiful
house I have ever seen.
I am very grateful
to you. You have made
me more than happy
and I promise to
give Quinne the best
of care and love.
Sincerely,
Susan Markley

In Palm Desert, California, in spring 1962, the former president met with his successor, John F. Kennedy.

Right: Eisenhower conferred with Johnson at the White House in August 1965.

The election of John F. Kennedy in 1960 discouraged Dwight Eisenhower. He believed that Kennedy's slim victory over Richard Nixon, his vice president for eight years, represented a repudiation of his administration's achievements. His gloom would grow after Kennedy's inauguration.

Eisenhower was startled by what he considered poor planning for the Bay of Pigs invasion of Castro-controlled Cuba, a disaster that took place in 1961, just months after Kennedy entered the White House. Eisenhower also thought that Kennedy's promise to put a man on the moon – made after the Bay of Pigs – pinned the country's nascent space effort to a single priority, the success of which was uncertain.

Lyndon Johnson, Kennedy's successor in the White House, presented Eisenhower different issues.

As a legendary backslapper, Johnson represented everything Eisenhower found distasteful about politicians. Eisenhower's pain at the LBJ treatment was more than figurative; before one meeting with Johnson, Eisenhower asked a friend to stand between the two of them. Eisenhower's bursitis was flaring and he winced at the prospect of Johnson's hale-fellow-well-met rituals.

In policy matters, Eisenhower and Johnson were closer. It was with Johnson, Senate minority leader in the late 1950s, that

President Eisenhower established the country's space program. In the 1960s Eisenhower supported President Johnson's decision to expand America's commitment of military assets to South Vietnam. In March 1965 he wrote Johnson endorsing the decision to send in combat troops. Eisenhower biographer Stephen Ambrose wrote that Johnson, little versed in foreign policy, was eager for Eisenhower's support of his initiatives in southeast Asia. Nevertheless, as the 1960s wore on, Eisenhower grew exasperated at what he considered Johnson's gradual approach in South Vietnam.

SOME ADVICE FOR A REPUBLICAN

In summer 1966, while actor Ronald Reagan was campaigning to become governor of California, he was vigorously backed by Freeman Gosden of Beverly Hills. Gosden had won fame with Charles Correll as the voices of "Amos 'n' Andy" on network radio. He worried that Reagan's foes were trying to connect him with the far-right John Birch Society and to paint him as anti-Semitic. Eisenhower replied to Gosden with this bit of political advice.

July 11, 1966

PERSONAL

Dear Freeman:

Your letter dated the seventh came in this morning, the eleventh. I suppose the Air Line strike is to blame. The picture is not yet here.

I'll call you later today, but this letter can be sort of "an aide memoir." Here I suggest that Reagan make arrangements to see that, at the first major press conference he holds, some individual question him about as follows:

"Mr. Reagan, I hear that you have disavowed any connection with the John Birch Society but, at the same time I've had reports that you are anti-Semitic. Do you have anything to say on this point?"

He answer could be as emphatic -- and as short -- as possible. For example:

"I've heard of this malicious accusation. It is **not** true. Anyone who repeats this rumor is guilty of a deliberate falsehood."

Then at another point in the conference he might say something like this:

"In this campaign I've been presenting to the public some of the things I want to do for California -- meaning for **all** the people of our State. I do not exclude any citizen from my concern and I make no distinctions among them on such invalid bases as color or creed."

PERSONAL

Something conveying this meaning might well be slipped into every talk -- such as "There are no 'minority' groups so far as I'm concerned. We are all Americans."

There are literally hundreds of ways for expressing the same idea.

I hope you've phoned Cliff about Haas and Hornby because Jim Murphy might be useful in bringing them into line.

Personally, I'd think that if Reagan has some good friend in the north who was formerly a Christopher supporter, such a person could talk confidentially with the two "reluctant" dragons to find out exactly what is bothering them. The best intermediary (provided he is from the north) would seem to be the State Chairman.

There is another approach that might be used. Whether or not Reagan has organized an "Advisory" or similar body I do not know. If he has, or is doing so, these two men could be invited to serve.

Again this is only one idea; many channels are open, not only to attract particular individuals, but to give a cosmopolitan or "broad spectrum" appearance to the campaign by enlisting the names and, if possible, the help of respected individuals throughout the State. And, very important, get some fine women on the staff and in every group set up.

Give him and Mrs. Reagan my warm regard and my earnest wishes for their success.

                           Devotedly,

Mr. Freeman Gosden
720 North Alpine Drive
Beverly Hills, California

In March 1967, after Reagan's election as California governor, he shared a laugh with the former president.

CRAZY ABOUT BARBECUES

In 1967 the former president forwarded a three-page position paper to his grandson, David, who was then facing a task daunting for any bachelor: preparing meat for dinner guests.

The letter written by the retired five-star general is full of specific instructions: potatoes peeled with strips not greater than a half-inch, for example.

Eisenhower's barbecue credentials were solid, the product of long experience. A 1940s photograph captured Ike and Mamie in full patio splendor – Mamie relaxing in an outdoor chair, Ike in barbecue apron, wielding a spatula. In 1954, a *Time* magazine correspondent followed the president to the convention of the National Association of Retail Grocers. He saw the chief executive distracted by the sight of several "shining machines" in which meat turned on spits over open flames.

"Brother, I'm just crazy about barbecues," the president said. "I love 'em."

When an executive of the D & W Manufacturing Co. offered to send Eisenhower a $400 "Barbecue King" model, the president said, "I'm afraid that is one gift I couldn't refuse." Whether the president actually took delivery is not reported.

By 1967, the former chief executive's advice to David was precise. Buy a prime cut if available, choice if not.

Pre-heat to 300 degrees.

Take out when the meat thermometer reaches 130 degrees.

And in conclusion, "Ice cream for dessert."

Facing page, top right: In the 1940s at Fort Lewis, Washington.

Dear David:

The enclosed is to buy a 3 or 4 rib beef roast. It will probably weigh from 6-9 pounds. While over the phone I said you should buy a roast labelled U.S.D.A. (U.S. Department of Agriculture) "choice," I have changed my mind.

You won't cook many roasts this summer so I think you should ask for the classification "prime." The Super Markets do not always carry this classification, but if you find difficulty in buying "prime" the "choice" will still be quite satisfactory. The classification will be stamped in purple on the meat itself.

I shall send along to you a meat thermometer. They usually register from about 130 to 190 degrees. The sharp end should be inserted in the middle of the roast from one side; do not let any part of it touch the bone.

To bake, first wipe off the roast with a damp cloth. Let it stand, outside the refrigerator, until it is room temperature. To estimate the time between when you put the meat in the oven and when you take it out, allow 20 minutes to the pound. This will provide a good guess as to when you should plan dinner, but for exact timing, trust the thermometer.

If you like the center quite rare allow the thermometer to get to 130 degrees only; should others like it fairly well done, save the outside cuts for him, or let the thermometer go to 140 degrees.

Pre-heat the oven to 300 degrees. Place roast in pan with rib-side down; fat up. Do not turn while cooking! When thermometer reaches 130 degrees take the pan out of oven and place roast on a warm platter at someplace where it will remain warm. It should stand about 20 minutes before carving. Use a very sharp knife, holding roast steady with a large fork. Cut slices quite thin and take off only the amount you estimate will be eaten.

(It is better to have to carve seconds when desired than to have some sliced meat left over. Whatever part of the roast remains should be wrapped in foil or in special ice box paper and placed in your refrigerator for serving cold later. There's no better cold snack than a rib itself.)

When the meat is placed on the platter, the gravy should be made at once.

Several steps:

Pour off and discard all but about <u>3 tablespoons of the melted fat.</u> Small pieces of the browned meat will stick to the bottom of the pan. Loosen them with the back of a knife, but leave them in pan.

Now, place pan on top of stove over very low fire. Put in 3 tablespoons of flour and keep stirring it so that the flour does not burn but all of it gets golden brown.

Remove from fire <u>momentarily</u> and pour in slowly abou 1 1/2 cups of very hot consomme or bouillon, stirring constantly u the whole is quite smooth. Put back on low fire. Keep stirring as the mixture comes to a boil. If the gravy thickens too much, stir a small amount of whole milk. When all is smooth, season to ser and keep hot until ready to serve.

With the roast I'd use string beans. Get about 1 1/2 lbs. They shou be washed, the ends nipped off, and, if fairly long, cut into two pi Get a small piece of ham(1/2 pound) to cook with them. Water onl to cover, no more.

Let them cook until tender. Drain, discarding ham. Put in a wa bowl and season to taste, adding a patty of butter or margarine.

I'd recommend mashed potatoes. Get 5-6 medium sized, peeling taking off narrow strips of peel, no more than 1/2 inch wide(Other you will waste so much you will have too little left.)

a ham base is just as good

Put in a pot with enough water to cover and a teaspoon of salt. When soft (but not mushy) drain well. Place the pan back on fire for one minute just to drive off moisture. Take off fire, crush with a wooden or wire potato masher. (I've used a big fork in my time), season with salt and fresh pepper and stir in whole milk, or thin cream, until nice and smooth. Place in a dish. Make a well in center and put in a pat of butter.

For salad, buy a couple of stalks of celery. Wash and cut up in usable pieces. Pile some ice on it until time to serve -- then drain and put on table.

Ice cream for dessert.

Make your pals wash the dishes!

Devotedly,

Mr. Dwight David Eisenhower II

P.S. Keep the thermometer and bring home to me next September.

When you go to the shop you'll want to buy: (I assume you have flour)
1 roast - "prime" if possible
a can of consomme or bouillon
1 or 2 good stalks of celery
1½ pounds of green or wax beans
small piece of ham or a ham bone
1 pint of good milk
6 medium potatoes
Enclosed : $20

Only five years into retirement, the former president had to confront his declining health. In 1965 he suffered a heart attack and soon after recovering began dispersing his cattle. About the same time, he traveled to Colorado and supervised the removal of the remains of his older son, Doud Dwight "Icky" Eisenhower – who had died as a young child in 1921 – and had them re-interred in the chapel on the grounds of the Eisenhower Library and Museum in Abilene.

In April 1968, he had yet another heart attack. The next month he was moved to Walter Reed Army Hospital in Washington. Another heart attack occurred in August.

On March 24, 1969, his heart began to fail. He received a visit from evangelist Billy Graham. He took a moment to dictate a brief note of appreciation to composer Irving Berlin.

On March 28, 1969, he died.

DDE

GETTYSBURG
PENNSYLVANIA 17325
Walter Reed Hospital
March 24, 1969

Dear Irving:

I have cajoled my doctors and nurses into letting me dictate this letter---it is a brief but very sincere note of thanks to you for the wonderful melodies you have created over the years.

A good part of my days here at Walter Reed are occupied with expert treatment by attentive doctors and nurses and some reading, but always with back-ground music. I have wanted you to know what pleasure you have brought to me not only during my recovery but for so many years. No music has meant so much to me as yours.

I hope all is well with you and yours---please do not bother to respond.

With warm regard to you and Mrs. Berlin in which Mrs. Eisenhower joins.

Cordially,

DDE.

To general Dwight D. Eisenhower,
with grateful appreciation for his wise counsel,
and loyal friendship through the years

from

Dick Nixon

Febuary 2, 196

Days after he was inaugurated as president in early 1969, Richard Nixon
paid a last visit to his old boss in the hospital.

According to his own instructions, Eisenhower's body was placed in a standard-issue soldier's coffin. It was taken to lie in state in the Capitol rotunda in Washington.

ACKNOWLEDGMENTS

Visitors to the Dwight D. Eisenhower Presidential Library and Museum in Abilene, Kansas, can count on good roads, great plains and world-class assistance from the staff.

Dan Holt, now retired as director of the library, and Karl Weissenbach, his successor as director, showed us every courtesy. Mack Teasley, executive director of the Eisenhower Foundation, welcomed our interest and provided support.

Library archivist James Leyerzapf, audiovisual archivist Kathy Struss and museum curator Dennis Medina brought forth materials we requested and, more important, produced other holdings we didn't know to ask about. Archives technician Chalsea Millner frequently anticipated our requests even before they occurred to us.

We thank them all.

— Brian Burnes and Monroe Dodd
May 2008

A statue of Eisenhower, dressed in his general's uniform, stands amid the grounds of the Eisenhower Museum and Library in Abilene. It faces the home in which he grew up.

INDEX

A

Abbott, Bud, and Costello, Lou, 132-133
Abilene High School, 9, 10, 12, 100, 177
American Battle Monuments Commission, 54, 57
Arden, Elizabeth, 166-167
Astaire, Fred, 184

B

baseball, 176-181
Berlin, Irving, 252
Blaik, Earl "Red," 105
Bolger, Ray, 169
Bradley, Omar, 72, 88, 94
Bristow, Joseph, 12
Brown, Joe E., 169
Bush, George H.W., 200
Byrd, Richard E., 136-137

C

Camp Colt, 40
Camp Meade, 40- 41, 101
captured Americans, 128-131
Churchill, Winston, 72, 77, 242-243
Clark, Mark, 20
civil rights, 138-157
Cochran, Jacqueline, 106
Columbia University, 99
concentration camps, 94-97
Conner, Fox, 53-56, 70
Cronkite, Walter, 238

D

D-Day (June 6, 1944), 78-84, 238-241
Diem, Ngo Dinh, 204-209
Dulles, John Foster, 210, 222-223

E

Eisenhower, Arthur 3, 5
Eisenhower, David, 159
Eisenhower, Doug Dwight "Icky," 36, 48, 49, 252, 257
Eisenhower Earl 3, 5
Eisenhower, Edgar, 3, 5, 7, 9-12
Eisenhower, John, 50, 58, 115, 250
Eisenhower, Mamie Geneva Doud, 23, 32-38, 54, 58, 112-113, 115, 158-159, 166-167, 213, 234, 237, 250-251
Eisenhower, Milton, 3, 5
Eisenhower, Paul 3
Eisenhower, Roy 3, 5
Elizabeth II, 164-165

F

Faubus, Orville, 148-149
Fitzgerald, F. Scott, 40
football, 100-105
Fort Leavenworth, 40, 54
Fort Sam Houston, 23, 32, 68
Fugate, Caril Ann, 170-171

G

Gardner, Ava, 184
Gilpin (Faust), Drew, 143
Graham, Billy, 144-147, 252
golf, 210-217
Goodpaster, Andrew, 223-224
Gosden, Freeman, 248

H

Hagerty, James, 214-215
Harding, Gladys, 22-31
Hazlett, Everett, "Swede," 12, 53, 132, 138, 210
Hoover, Herbert, 115-116
Horne, Lena, 169
Howe, Joseph, 12

I

interstate highway system, 200-203

J

Jackson, N. Stover, 8
Johnson, Lyndon, 179, 190, 196, 237, 246-247

K

Keel, Howard, 169
Kennedy, John F., 237, 246
King Jr., Martin Luther, 156
Khrushchev, Nikita, 222, 226
Korea, 118-119
Kruger, Jake, 22-23

L

Larsen, Don, 176, 180
Liberace, 169
Little, Lou, 102
Little Rock (Central High School), 148-153
Lodge Jr, Henry Cabot, 106

M

MacArthur, Douglas, 60-67, 70, 132, 234
Markley, Susan, 244-245
Marshall, George, 54, 68, 72. 78, 94
McCarthy, Joseph, 119, 124-127
Merrifield, Wes, 7, 19
Montgomery, Robert, 218-219
Moos, Malcolm, 230-231

N

Newcombe, Don, 176, 180
Nixon, Richard, 111, 15, 154, 179, 196, 234, 253
Norman, Ruby, 16-17, 19, 23, 32, 34, 100, 102

O

Outerbridge, William, 71

P

Panama Canal Zone, 53
Patton, George, 40, 94
Pearl Harbor, 68, 70, 71
Peck, Gregory, 184
Perkins, Anthony, 184
Pershing, John, 53, 56-57
Philippines, 62
Powers, Gary Francis, 222
Presley, Elvis, 162-163

R

Randolph, A. Phillip, 156
Rockne, Knute, 102
Robinson, Jackie, 154-155
Reagan, Ronald, 237, 248-249
Roosevelt, Franklin, 60, 73, 94
Rosenberg, Ethel and Julius, 119-123
Russell, Connie, 169
Ruth, Babe, 181

S

Simon, Richard L., 228-229
Snyder, Howard, 134, 210, 234
space, 188-199
Sputnik 190-193
Starkweather, Charles, 170-171
Steinberg, Jill, 160-161
Summersby, Kay, 74-77, 82-83, 90-92

T

Tinsley, Sophie, 140-142
transcontinental convoy, 42-47
Truman, Harry, 62, 139

U

U-2 spy plane, 222
unidentified flying objects, 172-175
U.S. Military Academy (West Point), 14-15, 18-21, 500, 100
USS Ward, 71

V

Vietnam, 204-209
von Braun, Wernher, 189

W

Wagner, Honus, 176
Wilkins, Roy, 156-157
Williams, Ralph, 230-231